A BOOK OF INSULT

A BOOK OF
INSULT

Edited by

PENELOPE FRITH

◆ B O O K ◆ B L O C K S ◆

This edition first published in 2004 by
Book Blocks, an imprint of
CRW Publishing Limited
69 Gloucester Crescent, London NW1 7EG

ISBN 1 904633 54 4

3 5 7 9 10 8 6 4 2

Editorial selection by Penelope Frith
Typeset in Great Britain by Antony Gray
Printed and bound in China by Imago

Contents

❧ If in the last few years you haven't discarded a major opinion, or acquired a new one, check your pulse. You may be dead.

FRANK GELETT BURGESS (1866–1951)

Introduction

✌ Evolution is a cruel process. Relentlessly, generation by generation, it eliminates those who are less successful at reproduction – usually the weak and less well-armed. This may explain why impugning the size or friskiness of a man's sexual equipment seems to strike at the very heart of his genetic purpose. For sound Darwinian reasons we hominids have always been at our most inventive when it comes to devising means of killing each other.

Insults are similarly creative and have as long a history. Their purpose is twofold – and is much more complex than mere verbal aggression, so often little more than an inarticulate scream that is a preliminary to grievous bodily harm. Insults, on the other hand, have a double action. Of course they are designed to wound, for many are piercingly malicious and all the more effective for their (occasional) unforgivable accuracy. But in addition to the formal content of the insult, there is another bruising message. It is this: to demonstrate the linguistic skills and quickness of wit of their perpetrator compared to the victim. Look, the inventor of a witty insult is saying, not only are you a nasty piece of work but you have only a fraction of the intellect and cleverness of me, your superior in all respects. That is why the most elegant bitcheries are to be found among the cohorts of writers and other wordsmiths.

These people, notoriously riven with jealousy, are also likely to be professionally deft with the ultimate weapon of mass destruction: language itself.

Cavilling critics &
other literary parasites

❧ As for you, little envious prigs, snarling bastard puny critics, you'll soon have railed your last: go hang yourselves.

FRANÇOIS RABELAIS (c.1494–c.1553)
French satirist

❧ Dr Donne's verses are like the Peace of God, for they pass all understanding.

JAMES I (1566–1625)
on John Donne

ॐ This dodipoue, this didopper . . . thou arrant butter whore, thou cotqueane and scrattop of scoldes . . . you kitchin-stuff wrangler!

THOMAS NASHE (1567–1601)
on Gabriel Harvey

ॐ Our language sinks under him.

JOSEPH ADDISON (1672–1719)
on the poetry of John Milton

ॐ A lewd vegetarian.

CHARLES KINGSLEY (1819–1875)
English author, on Percy Bysshe Shelley

❧ Vain Nashe, railing Nashe, cracking Nashe, bibbing Nashe, baggage Nashe . . . roguish Nashe . . . the swish-swash of the press, the bum of impudency, the shambles of beastliness . . . the toadstool of the realm . . .

GABRIEL HARVEY (c.1550–1630)
on Thomas Nashe

❧ They who write ill, and they who
ne'er durst write,
Turn critics out of mere revenge and spite.

JOHN DRYDEN (1631–1700)
English poet

❧ Paradise Lost is one of the books which the reader admires and lays down, and forgets to take up again. Its perusal is a duty rather than a pleasure.

DR SAMUEL JOHNSON (1709–1784)
English author and lexicographer,
on the work of John Milton

❧ This obscure, eccentric and disgusting poem.

FRANÇOIS MARIE AROUET DE VOLTAIRE
(1694–1773)
French philosopher and writer,
on a work by John Milton

A fly can sting a horse and make it wince, but a fly is but a fly and a horse is still a horse.

DR SAMUEL JOHNSON (1709–1784)
on critics

A monster gibbering shrieks, and gnashing imprecations against mankind – tearing down all shreds of modesty, past all sense of manliness and shame, filthy in word, filthy in thought, furious, raging, obscene.

WILLIAM MAKEPEACE THACKERAY (1811–1863)
English novelist, on Jonathan Swift

❧ I do not like you, Dr Fell
The reason why, I cannot tell.
But this I know, and know full well,
I do not like you, Dr Fell.

ANONYMOUS

❧ Sir, he was dull in company, dull in his
closet, dull everywhere. He was dull in a
new way, and that made many people think
him great. He was a mechanical poet.

DR SAMUEL JOHNSON (1709–1784)
on the poet Thomas Gray

⚞ Sir, there is no settling the precedency between a louse and a flea.

DR SAMUEL JOHNSON, (1709–1784)
verse of Robert Herrick and Christopher Smart

⚞ The verses, when they were written, resembled nothing so much as spoonfuls of boiling oil, ladled out by a fiendish monkey at an upstairs window upon such of the passers-by whom the wretch had a grudge against.

LYTTON STRACHEY (1880–1932)
English biographer, on Alexander Pope

≋ Casts of manure a wagon-load around
    To raise a simple daisy from the ground;
    Uplifts the club of Hercules, for what?
    To crush a butterfly, or brain a gnat!

JOHN WOLCOT (1738–1819)
English satirist, on Dr Samuel Johnson

≋ Johnson made the most brutal speeches to
living persons; for though he was good-
natured at bottom, he was ill-natured at top.
He loved to dispute to show his superiority.
If his opponents were weak, he told them
they were fools; if they vanquished him, he
was scurrilous.

HORACE WALPOLE (1717–1797)
English writer

He was a liar and a cheat; he paid no regard to truth, nor to any kind of moral obligation.

ROBERT SOUTHEY (1774–1843)
English poet, on Percy Bysshe Shelley

Have you got Boswell's most absurd enormous book? . . . The more one learns of Johnson, the more preposterous assemblage he appears of strong sense, of the lowest bigotry and prejudices, of pride, brutality, fretfulness and vanity – and Boswell is the ape of most of his faults, without a grain of his sense. It is the story of a mountebank and his zany.

HORACE WALPOLE (1717–1797)

❧ Thou eunuch of language . . . thou pimp of gender . . . murderous accoucheur of infant learning . . . thou pickle-herring in the puppet show of nonsense.

ROBERT BURNS (1759–1796)
Scottish poet, on a critic

❧ Here is Jonny Keats' piss-a-bed poetry . . . No more Keats, I entreat: flay him alive; if some of you don't I must skin him myself: there is no bearing the drivelling idiotism of the Mankin.

GEORGE GORDON, LORD BYRON (1788–1824)
English poet

❧ His manners are 99 in a 100 singularly repulsive.

> SAMUEL TAYLOR COLERIDGE (1772–1834)
> *English poet, on William Hazlitt*

❧ Fricassee of dead dog . . . A truly unwise little book. The kind of man that Keats was gets ever more horrible to me. Force of hunger for pleasure of every kind, and want of all other force – such a soul, it would once have been very evident, was a chosen 'vessel of Hell'.

> THOMAS CARLYLE (1795–1881)
> *Scottish historian, on the* Life of Keats
> *by Monckton Milnes*

❧ Mr Shelley is a very vain man; and like most
vain men, he is but half instructed in
knowledge and less than half disciplined
in reasoning powers; his vanity has
been his ruin.

QUARTERLY REVIEW

❧ Let simple Wordsworth chime his
childish verse,
And brother Coleridge lull the babe
at nurse.

GEORGE GORDON, LORD BYRON (1788–1824)

~ Rogers is not very well . . . Don't you know he has produced a couplet? When he is delivered of a couplet, with infinite labour and pain, he takes to his bed, has straw laid down, the knocker tied up, expects his friends to call and make enquiries, and the answer at the door invariably is 'Mr Rogers and his little couplet are as well as can be expected.'

SYDNEY SMITH (1771–1845)
English clergyman and essayist

~ A great cow-full of ink!

GUSTAVE FLAUBERT (1820–1880)
French novelist, on Georges Sand

ɶ Oh, Amos Cottle – Phoebus, what a name
To fill the speaking trump of future fame!
Oh, Amos Cottle, for a moment think
What meagre profits spring from pen
                                      and ink!

GEORGE GORDON, LORD BYRON (1788–1824)
on the Poet Laureate

ɶ A denaturalised being who, having
exhausted every species of sensual
gratification, and drained the cup of sin
to its bitterest dregs, is resolved to show
that he is no longer human, even in his
frailties, but a cool, unconcerned fiend.

JOHN STYLES
on Lord Byron

Byron! – he would be all forgotten today if he had lived to be a florid old gentleman with iron-grey whiskers, writing very long, very able letters to The Times about the Repeal of the Corn Laws.

MAX BEERBOHM (1872–1956)
English writer and caricaturist

A mere ulcer; a sore from head to foot; a poor devil so completely flayed that there is not a square inch of healthy flesh on his carcass; an overgrown pimple, sore to the touch.

QUARTERLY REVIEW
on William Hazlitt

❧ Dank, limber verses, stuft with
                    lakeside sedges,
And propt with rotten stakes from
                    rotten hedges.

WALTER SAVAGE LANDOR (1775–1864)
English writer, on William Wordsworth

❧ Wordsworth has left a bad impression
wherever he visited in town by his egotism,
vanity and bigotry.

JOHN KEATS (1795–1821)
English poet

For prolixity, thinness, endless dilution, it excels all the other speech I had heard from mortals . . . The languid way in which he gives you a handful of numb unresponsive fingers is very significant.

THOMAS CARLYLE (1795–1881)
on William Wordsworth

His imagination resembled the wings of an ostrich. It enabled him to run, but not to soar.

THOMAS BABINGTON, LORD MACAULAY
(1800–1859)
English historian and poet

  ❦   . . . One who would creep and botanise
upon his mother's grave.

WILLIAM WORDSWORTH (1770–1850)
on a fellow nature poet

  ❦ A weak, diffusive, weltering, ineffectual
man . . . never did I see such apparatus
got ready for thinking, and so little thought.
He mounts scaffolding, pulleys and tackle,
gathers all the tools in the neighbourhood
with labour, with noise, demonstration,
precept, abuse, and sets – three bricks.

THOMAS CARLYLE (1795–1881)
on Samuel Taylor Coleridge

❧ Great literature is the creation, for the most part, of disreputable characters, many of whom looked rather seedy, some of whom were drunken blackguards, a few of whom were swindlers or perpetual borrowers, rowdies, gamblers or slaves to a drug.

ALEXANDER HARVEY (1799–1876)
Scottish biographer

❧ What does pain me exceedingly is that you should write so badly. These verses are execrable, and I am shocked that you seem unable to perceive it.

EDMUND GOSSE (1845–1928)
English poet and critic, to Robert Nichols

∝ One must have a heart of stone to read the death of little Nell without laughing.

OSCAR WILDE (1856–1900)
British dramatist and poet, on
Charles Dickens's The Old Curiosity Shop

∝ . . . Mr Swinburne; and lo! The Bacchanal screams, the sterile Dolores sweats, serpents dance, men and women wrench, wriggle, and foam in an endless alliteration of heated and meaningless word.

ROBERT BUCHANAN (1841–1901)
English poet and novelist

❧ The critic's symbol should be the tumble-bug; he deposits his egg in someone else's dung, otherwise he could not hatch it.

MARK TWAIN (1835–1910)
American writer

❧ I could readily see in Emerson . . . a gaping flaw. It was the insinuation that had he lived in those days when the world was made, he might have offered some valuable suggestions.

HERMAN MELVILLE (1819–1891)
American writer

  ❧ With the single exception of Homer, there is
no eminent writer, not even Sir Walter
Scott, whom I can despise as entirely as I
despise Shakespeare when I measure my
mind against his. The intensity of my
impatience with him occasionally reaches
such a pitch, that it would positively be a
relief to me to dig him up and throw stones
at him . . .

GEORGE BERNARD SHAW (1856–1950)
Anglo-Irish dramatist

  ❧ A louse in the locks of literature.

ALFRED, LORD TENNYSON (1809–1892)
English poet, on the critic Churton Collins

℞ The way Bernard Shaw believes in himself is very refreshing in these atheistic days when so many people believe in no God at all.

ISRAEL ZANGWILL (1864–1926)
English novelist, in reply to Shaw on Shakespeare

℞ What is a writer but a schmuck with a typewriter?

JACK WARNER (1892–1978)
film producer and director, on screenwriters

℞ The work of a queasy undergraduate scratching his pimples . . .

VIRGINIA WOOLF (1882–1941)
English novelist, on James Joyce

⁍ We know of no spectacle so ridiculous as the British public in one of its periodical fits of morality.

THOMAS BABINGTON, LORD MACAULAY
(1800–1859)

⁍ I merely informed him, in language of the strictest reserve, that he was a hoary-headed and toothless baboon, who, first lifted into notice on the shoulder of Carlyle, now spits and splutters from a filthier platform of his own finding and fouling. That's all I've said.

A. C. SWINBURNE (1837–1909)
English poet, on Ralph Waldo Emerson

ℂ I'm afraid that something I once wrote
about Mr Arnold Bennett in a critical way so
prejudiced me against him that I never read
another word he wrote.

OLIVER HERFORD (1863–1935)

ℂ It is written by a man with a diseased mind
and soul so black that he would even
obscure the darkness of hell.

SENATOR REED SMOOT (1862–1941)
on James Joyce's Ulysses

❧ My God, what a clumsy olla putrida James Joyce is! Nothing but old fags and cabbage-stumps of quotations from the Bible and the rest, stewed in the juice of deliberate, journalistic dirty-mindedness.

D. H. LAWRENCE (1885–1930)
English poet and novelist

❧ This is not a novel to be tossed aside lightly. It should be thrown with great force.

DOROTHY PARKER (1893–1967)
American writer

✿ A combination of Little Nell and
  Lady Macbeth.

ALEXANDER WOOLCOTT (1887–1943)
on Dorothy Parker

✿ The jelly-boned swine, the slimy, the
  belly-wriggling invertebrates, the miserable
  sodding rotters, the flaming sods, the
  snivelling, dribbling, dithering, palsied,
  pulseless lot that make up England today.

D. H. LAWRENCE (1885–1930)

The great Gaels of Ireland,
The ones whom God made mad.
For all their wars are merry,
And all their songs are sad.

ANONYMOUS IRISH BARD

For the young Gaels of Ireland
Are the lads that drive me mad,
For half their words need footnotes
And half their rhymes are bad.

ARTHUR GUITERMAN

There is so much nastiness in modern literature that I like to write stories that contain nothing worse than a little innocent murdering.

EDGAR WALLACE (1875–1932)
English novelist and playwright

Q: How many authors does it take to change a light-bulb?
A: Ten. One to do the job and nine to bitch and whinge that by rights it should have been them doing it.

ANONYMOUS

❧ He was able to turn an unplotted,
unworkable manuscript into an
unplotted and unworkable manuscript
with a lot of sex.

TOM VOLPE
on Harold Robbins

❧ Publishers are often sent truly dire material for
consideration. This rejection slip (attributed to
Eugene Field) was in response to a particularly
soppy poem called 'Why do I live?'

The answer: Because you sent your poem
by mail.

❧ If you want to get rich from writing, write the sort of thing that's read by persons who move their lips when reading.

DON MARQUIS (1878–1937)
American writer

❧ Everywhere I go I am asked if university stifles writers. My opinion is that it doesn't stifle enough of them.

FLANNERY O'CONNOR (1924–1964)
American writer

Bilious nights at the movies & on stage

❧ Spending time in theatres produces fornication, intemperance, and every kind of impurity.

ST JOHN CHRYSOSTOM (c.347–407)

❧ Shakespeare, Madam, is obscene, and, thank God, we are sufficiently advanced to have found it out.

ANONYMOUS
quoted by Frances Trollope (1780–1863),
English novelist

∾ To the King's Theatre, where we saw
Midsummer Night's Dream, which I had
never seen before, nor shall ever again, for
it is the most insipid, ridiculous play that
ever I saw in my life.

SAMUEL PEPYS (1633–1703)
English diarist and politician

∾ There is a total extinction of all taste: our
authors are vulgar, gross, illiberal;
the theatre swarms with wretched
translations, and ballad operas, and we
have nothing new but improving abuse.

HORACE WALPOLE (1717–1797)
English writer

ॐ There is an upstart crow beautified with our feathers. That with his tyger's heart wrapt in a players's hide, supposes he is as well able to bombast out a blank verse as the best of you; and being an absolute Johannes Factotum, is, in his own conceit, the only Shakescene in a country.

ROBERT GREENE (1558–1592)
English dramatist, on his contemporary
William Shakespeare

ॐ Was there ever such stuff as a great part of Shakespeare? Only one must not say so! But what think you – What? Is there not much sad stuff? What? – What?

GEORGE III (1738–1820)

ॐ Players, Sir! I look on them as no better than creatures set upon tables and joint-stools to make faces and produce laughter, like dancing dogs.

DR SAMUEL JOHNSON (1709–1784)
English author and lexicographer

ॐ Is it a stale remark to say that I have constantly found the interest excited at a playhouse to bear an exact inverse proportion to the price paid for admission?

CHARLES LAMB (1775–1834)
English essayist

∝ Another week's rehearsal with WSG & I should have gone raving mad. I had already ordered some straw for my hair.

SIR ARTHUR SULLIVAN (1842–1900)
English composer, on Sir William Schwenck Gilbert, of the Gilbert and Sullivan musicals

∝ No one can fully appreciate the fatuity of human nature until he has spent some time in a box office.

ST JOHN ERVINE (1883–1971)
American playwright

≈ A boring man is said to have sought out the actor John Barrymore at a smart but tedious party.

'It's good to see you, Mr Barrymore,' he said, 'for you are the first person I've met tonight who is worth talking to.'

'I must say,' Barrymore replied, 'that you are more fortunate than I.'

≈ My Dear Sir,
I have read your play.
Oh, my dear Sir.
Yours Faithfully

SIR HERBERT BEERBOHM TREE (1853–1917)
English actor and theatre manager

ॐ A freakish homunculus germinated outside lawful procreation.

HENRY ARTHUR JONES (1851–1929)
on Bernard Shaw

ॐ Funny without being vulgar.

SIR HERBERT BEERBOHM TREE (1853–1917)
describing himself as Hamlet

ॐ Your skin has been acting at any rate.

W. S. GILBERT (1836–1911)
English librettist, to a sweating
Sir Herbert Beerbohm Tree

☘ You had to stand in line to hate him.

HEDDA HOPPER
on Harry Cohn

☘ He made a fortune by pretending to shrink
from publicity, because he knew that was
the best way of obtaining it.

JAMES FAIRLIE
Sunday Express, *on J. M. Barrie*

☘ KATHERINE HEPBURN (to John Barrymore):
Thank goodness I don't have to act with you
any more.
BARRYMORE: I didn't know you ever had,
darling.

❧ Laved by the gentle Avon, surrounded by lawns dotted with trees, the crouching red-brick outline of the Memorial Theatre suggests a courageous and partially successful attempt to disguise a gasworks as a racquet-court.

PETER FLEMING
Spectator

❧ A day away from Tallulah Bankhead is like a month in the country.

ANONYMOUS
on Tallulah Bankhead

ళ Chaplin's genius was in comedy. He had no
sense of humour.

LITA GREY
on her ex-husband Charlie Chaplin

ళ You should cross yourself when you say
his name.

MARLENE DIETRICH
on Orson Welles

ళ I deny that I said that actors are like cattle.
I said they should be treated like cattle.

ALFRED HITCHCOCK (1899–1980)
British film director

❧ By an ingenious camera treatment,
Mr Bogart's face is not seen until the
picture has run for an hour. One or two
other stars might try this.

P. L. MANNOCK
Daily Herald

❧ Gore Vidal once memorably described a
film producer, notorious for his low taste,
as 'so desperate that he scraped the top
of the barrel.'

❧ He has the compassion of an icicle . . .

S. J. PERELMAN
on Groucho Marx

≈ What really made Behan a household name in 1956 was being the first person to appear drunk and incapable on television.

HILARY SPURLING
Observer, *on Brendan Behan*

≈ The nearest we are ever likely to get to a human Mickey Mouse.

GRAHAM GREENE (1904–1991)
English Novelist on Fred Astaire

≈ He cried at all his own weddings – and with reason.

LAUREN BACALL
on Humphrey Bogart

❧ Daphne du Maurier is the dream novelist of film producers. They don't even have to improve on her books when they film them because she knows more clichés than any or all of them.

RICHARD WINNINGTON

❧ Katherine Hepburn runs the whole gamut of emotions – from A to B.

DOROTHY PARKER (1893–1967)
American writer

❧ The closest thing to the Roseanne Barr singing the national Anthem was my cat being neutered.

JOHNNY CARSON

෯ ... she toted a breast like a man totes
a gun.

GRAHAM GREENE (1904–1991)
on Jean Harlow

෯ The most swollen-headed, vainglorious
nincompoops in existence. Dirty little
£5-a-week fellers.

SAM HARRIS
on critics

෯ He got a reputation as a great actor just by
thinking hard about the next line.

KING VIDOR (1894–1982)
film director, on Gary Cooper

∾ Directing her was like directing Lassie.
You needed fourteen takes to get one of
them right.

OTTO PREMINGER
on Marilyn Monroe

∾ I am distressed that Mr Ustinov thought
my opinion of *The Young and the Fair*
was expressed too flippantly. I should like
to assure him, however, that my leaving at
the end of the second act was intended as a
serious piece of dramatic criticism.

STEPHEN BONE
writing to The Radio Times

☙ Mr Stewart Grainger appears as Paganini and pretends to play the violin. There is something agricultural about Mr Grainger's fiddling. He appears to be sawing wood with one hand and milking a cow with the other.

ELSPETH GRANT
writer

☙ You could never put Coop in a small hat and get your money back.

RICHARD ZANUCK
on Gary Cooper

He was once Slightly in Peter Pan, and has been wholly in Peter Pan ever since.

KENNETH TYNAN
on Noël Coward

Men of every age flocked around her like gulls round a council tip.

JOHN CAREY
Sunday Times, *on Diana Cooper*

Lillian Gish . . . comes on stage as if she'd been sent for to sew rings on the new curtains.

MRS PAT CAMPBELL (1865–1940)
English–Italian actress

❦ He had the acting talents of the average wardrobe.

CLYDE JEAVONS AND JEREMY PASCALL
on Rudolph Valentino

❦ One of my chief regrets during my years in the theatre is that I couldn't sit in the audience and watch me act.

JOHN BARRYMORE (1882–1942)

❦ When I saw one of his pictures I wanted to quit the business.

KING VIDOR (1894–1982)
on Cecil B. de Mille

❧ Joan Crawford drank 120-proof vodka all the time she was filming and still managed to block the lighting and cast dark shadows on her co-stars' faces.

SHEILA GRAHAM

❧ Surely no one but a mother could have loved Bette Davis at the height of her career.

BRIAN AHERNE
British actor

❧ She's not even an actress, only a trollop.

GLORIA SWANSON
on Lana Turner

❧ Veteran actor Ernest Thesiger says he was shopping in a West End store when a woman rushed up to him and said breathlessly, 'Excuse me, you were Ernest Thesiger, weren't you?'

NORAH ALEXANDER

❧ I always said that I'd like Barrymore's acting till the cows came home. Well, ladies and gentlemen, last night the cows came home.

Review by
GEORGE JEAN NATHAN (1882–1958)

❧ Cecil B. de Mille,
   Rather against his will,
   Was persuaded to leave Moses
   Out of *The Wars of the Roses*.

NICHOLAS BENTLEY
British artist and writer

❧ A friend once said that Cocteau discussed
   his own colds as if they were railway
   disasters.

RICHARD HOLMES
The Times, *on Jean Cocteau*

❧ What a change to go to a nice clean show
    (such a nice clean show, my dears),
And to see the vast and impersonal cast
    march past to deafening cheers.
It's not quite art or terribly smart, but
    dowagers weep in the stalls.
And I really can't see why the man next to
    me repeatedly said it was *****!

CHRISTOPHER SALTMARSHE
from Cavalcade for the General, on Noël Coward

❧ His life was a fifty-year trespass against good
taste.

LESLIE MALLORY
on Errol Flynn

◈ Clark is the sort of guy, if you say 'Hiya Clark, how are ya?' – he's stuck for an answer.

AVA GARDNER (1922–1990)
on Clark Gable

◈ He let opium choose his friends.

CYRIL CONNOLLY (1903–1975)
English critic, on Jean Cocteau

◈ He would not blow his nose without moralising on conditions in the handkerchief industry.

CYRIL CONNOLLY (1903–1975)
on George Orwell

❧ Working with her was like being hit over the head with a Valentine card.

CHRISTOPHER PLUMMER
on Julie Andrews

❧ Joan Collins is a commodity who would sell her own bowel movements

ANTHONY NEWLEY
(one of her ex-husbands)

❧ Academics rush to recite the names of her husbands like bright kids rattling off their multiplication tables.

BRENDA MADDOX
on Elizabeth Taylor

❧ Vic Oliver – if only his violin was as old
as his jokes.

WILFRED PICKLES (1905–1978)
English comic actor

❧ The best time I ever had with Joan Crawford
was when I pushed her down the stairs in
Whatever Happened to Baby Jane.

BETTE DAVIS (1908–1989)

❧ Copulation was, I'm sure, Marilyn's
uncomplicated way of saying thank you.

NUNNALLY JOHNSON
on Marilyn Monroe

❧ Television is a device that permits people who haven't anything to do watch people who can't do anything.

FRED ALLEN (1894–1956)
American radio comedian

❧ Say anything you want about me, but you make fun of my picture and you'll regret it the rest of your fat, midget life.

JOSHUA LOGAN
to Truman Capote

♺ Frank Sinatra, nearing retirement (again), had a tour of Australia marred by ill-natured and heavy-handed security arrangements. In fact they were so clumsy that a fan, keen to get an autograph was manhandled by the black-suited bodyguards and as a result was so irritated that he actually hit out at the great man. 'At last,' ran a story in the local paper, 'the fan hits the shit.'

Unknown Australian journalist

♺ Charlotte Rampling – a poor actress who mistakes creepiness for sensuality.

JOHN SIMON

❧ Television – the bland leading the bland.

ANONYMOUS

❧ Television – a medium. So called because it is neither rare nor well done.

ERNIE KOVACS (1919–1962)
TV comedian

❧ Television – chewing gum for the eyes.

FRANK LLOYD WRIGHT (1869–1959)
American architect

If music be the food
of invective . . .

❧ He was a fiddler, and consequently a rogue.

DR SAMUEL JOHNSON (1709–1784)
English author and lexicographer

❧ . . . others, when the bag-pipe sings in the
nose,
Cannot contain their urine.

WILLIAM SHAKESPEARE (1564–1616)
English dramatist, The Merchant of Venice

❧ Swans sing before they die; 'twere no bad
thing should certain persons die before
they sing.

SAMUEL TAYLOR COLERIDGE (1772–1834)
English poet

⍋ MOZART (*responding to a request for advice on composing a symphony from a precocious youngster*): You are still very young. Why not begin with ballads?
YOUTH: But you composed symphonies when you were only ten years old.
MOZART: True – but I didn't ask how.

WOLFGANG AMADEUS MOZART (1756–1791)
Austrian composer

⍋ Rossini would have been a great composer if his teacher had spanked him enough on his backside.

LUDWIG VAN BEETHOVEN (1770–1827)
German composer

❧ Wagner's music is better than it sounds.

MARK TWAIN (1835–1910)
American writer

❧ Is Wagner a human being at all? Is he not rather a disease?

FRIEDRICH NIETZSCHE (1844–1900)
German philosopher

❧ I love Wagner, but the music I prefer is that of a cat hung up by its tail outside a window and trying to stick to the panes of glass by its claws.

CHARLES BAUDELAIRE (1821–1867)
French poet

✀ I like Wagner's music better than any other music. It is so loud that one can talk the whole time without people hearing what one says.

OSCAR WILDE (1856–1900)
British dramatist and poet

✀ Perhaps it was because Nero played the fiddle, they burned Rome.

OLIVER HERFORD (1863–1935)

✀ He knew music was Good, but it didn't sound right.

GEORGE ADE (1866–1944)
American playwright

❧   Hell is full of musical amateurs.
       Music is the brandy of the damned.

GEORGE BERNARD SHAW (1856–1950)
Anglo–Irish dramatist

❧ Music invented for the torture of imbeciles.

HENRY VAN DYKE
on jazz

❧ Calls himself a violinist? He didn't even
    tell one gag.

COMEDIAN TED RAY
*on Yehudi Menuhin, Royal
Command Variety Show*

❧ At the invitation of the Redditch Friends of Music, the BBC Midland Light Orchestra left the studio in Birmingham on Friday evening to make one of its all-too-frequent public appearances.

REDDITCH INDICATO

❧ Modern music is three farts and a raspberry, orchestrated.

SIR JOHN BARBIROLLI (1899–1970)
British conductor

❧ The catch of the day was hepatitis.

HENRY YOUNGMAN

❧ Prince looks like a dwarf who's been dipped
in a bucket of pubic hair.

BOY GEORGE
on the artist formerly known as Prince

❧ . . . Elvis was no more than a horrible,
and horribly uncomplicated, embodiment
of American Success . . .

MARTIN AMIS
on Elvis Presley

❧ The Sydney Opera House looks as if it is
something that has crawled out the sea
and is up to no good.

BEVERLEY NICHOLS

ॐ I occasionally play works by contemporary
composers and for two reasons. First to
discourage the composer from writing any
more and secondly to remind myself how
much I appreciate Beethoven.

JASCHA HEIFETZ

ॐ The master bedroom – black suede walls,
crimson carpets and curtains, 81 square feet
of bed with mortuary headboard and
speckled armrests. On the bed lies Elvis
himself, propped up like a big fat woman
recovering from some operation on her
reproductive organs.

ALBERT GOLDMAN
on Elvis Presley

❧ He has van Gogh's ear for music.

ORSON WELLES
on Donny Osmond

❧ The baked potatoes looked as if they had been excreted by a buffalo.

BRIAN SEWELL
English art critic

❧ Wagner has beautiful moments, but awful quarter hours.

GIOACCHINO ROSSINI (1792–1868)
Italian operatic composer

❧ Whenever I ate with Ian at Goldeneye the food was so abominable that I used to cross myself before I took a mouthful. Stewed guavas and coconut cream, salt fish and ackee fruit. I used to say, 'Ian, it tastes like armpits.' And all the time there was old Ian smacking his lips and for more while his guests remembered all those delicious meals he had put in his books.

NOËL COWARD
on dining with Ian Fleming, author of the James Bond novels

Poisonous paintings
& dismal daubs

❧ Michelangelo was an excellent man, but he knew nothing about painting.

EL GRECO (1541–1614)
Spanish painter

❧ They are produced as if by throwing handsful of white and blue and red at the canvas, letting what chance to stick, stick, and then shadowing in some forms to make the appearance of a picture.

LITERARY GAZETTE
on William Turner

❧ A tortoise-shell cat having a fit in a
   platter of tomatoes.

MARK TWAIN (1835–1910)
American writer, on a
painting by William Turner

❧ The new French School is simply
   putrescence and decomposition. There
   is a man named Monet, to whose studio I
   was taken, whose pictures are for the most
   part, mere scrawls.

D. G. ROSSETTI (1828–1882)
English painter and poet, on the Impressionists

∂ If the old masters had labelled their fruit,
  one wouldn't be so likely to mistake pears
  for turnips.

MARK TWAIN (1835–1910)
American writer

∂ Mr Whistler has always spelt art with a
  capital 'I'.

OSCAR WILDE (1856–1900)
*British dramatist and poet, on
James McNeill Whistler*

  ❧ I never saw anything so impudent on the walls of any exhibition, in any country, as last year in London. It was a daub professing to be a 'harmony in pink and white' (or some such nonsense); absolute rubbish, and which had taken about quarter of an hour to scrawl or daub – it had no pretence to be called painting.

JOHN RUSKIN (1819–1900)
English author and art critic, on James McNeill Whistler's Symphony in Grey and Green

  ❧ It made me look as if I was straining a stool.

SIR WINSTON CHURCHILL (1874–1965)
British prime minister, on the portrait of him by Graham Sutherland

℞ Of course we all know that Morris was a wonderful all-round man, but the act of walking round him has always tired me.

MAX BEERBOHM (1872–1956)
English writer and caricaturist, on William Morris

℞ The English public takes no interest in a work of art until it is told that the work in question is immoral.

OSCAR WILDE (1856–1900)

℞ If my husband would ever meet a woman on the street who looked like the women in his paintings, he would fall over in a dead faint.

MRS PABLO PICASSO

❧   Good Mr Fortune, A.R.A.,
    Rejoiced in twenty sons,
    But even there he failed, they say,
    To get a likeness once.

G. R. HAMILTON
imitating Lucullus

❧ Epstein is a great sculptor. I wish he would
  wash, but I believe Michelangelo never did,
  so I suppose it is part of the tradition.

EZRA POUND (1885–1972)
American poet

∾ Abstract art? A product of the untalented, sold by the unprincipled to the utterly bewildered.

AL CAPP (1909–1979)
cartoonist creator of Li'l Abner

∾ I will fight to the last drop of my blood to have this figure removed. It is a question of art versus decency, and I am not going to allow my wife to be insulted.

THE MAYOR OF BLACKBURN IN 1934
on a copy of the Venus de Milo

❧ The Art Gallery, which belongs to
Bournemouth, is the most extraordinary
shrine of absolute bad taste that exists
in the whole of Great Britain. It should
certainly be preserved intact.

GEOFFREY GRIGSON
on the Russell-Cotes Art Gallery

❧ Of all the cants which are canted in this
canting world, though the cant of
hypocrisy may be the worst, the cant
of criticism is the most tormenting.

LAURENCE STERNE (1713–1768)
English novelist

Intellect impugned

⚞ A lover of himself, without any rival.

MARCUS TULLIUS CICERO (106–43 BC)
Roman orator, statesman and man of letters

⚞ Ye blind guides, which strain at a gnat,
and swallow a camel.

MATTHEW 3:7

⚞ You beat your pate, and fancy wit will come:
Knock as you please, there's nobody at
home.

ALEXANDER POPE (1688–1744)
English poet

❧ Barmy froth.

Traditional sixteenth-century insult

❧ Take from him his sophisms, futilities and
incomprehensibilities and what remains?
His foggy mind.

THOMAS JEFFERSON (1743–1826)
American president, on Plato

❧ The more I read him, the less I wonder
that they poisoned him.

THOMAS BABINGTON, LORD MACAULAY
(1800–1859)
English historian and poet, on Socrates

❧ His mind was a kind of extinct sulphur-pit.

THOMAS CARLYLE (1795–1881)
Scottish historian, on Napoleon III

❧ Take egotism out, and you would castrate
the benefactors.

RALPH WALDO EMERSON (1803–1882)
American essayist and philosopher

❧ A Byzantine logothete.

THEODORE ROOSEVELT (1858–1919)
American president, on Woodrow Wilson

A philosopher will not believe what he sees because he is too busy speculating about what he does not see.

LE BOYVER DE FONTENELLE (1657–1757)
French author

His mind is a muskeg of mediocrity.

JOHN MACNAUGHTON

His mind was like a soup dish – wide and shallow: it could hold a small amount of nearly anything, but the slightest jarring spilled the soup into somebody's lap.

IRVING STONE (1903–1989)
American author, on William Jennings Bryan

❧ Whatever women do they must do twice as well as men to be thought half as good. Luckily, this is not difficult.

CHARLOTTE WHITTON (1896–1975)
Mayor of Ottawa

❧ My position, sir, does not allow me to argue with you. But if ever it came to a choice of weapons, I should choose grammar.

ANONYMOUS
*quoting a headwaiter's reponse to abuse
from a subliterate customer*

❧ He was always bold, clear, concise, cultured, forceful, graceful, classical, eloquent and wrong.

IAN MACKAY
on Dean Inge

❧ Sir, you are like a pin, but without either its head or its point.

DOUGLAS WILLIAM JERROLD (1803–1857)
American editor

ও Your manuscript is both good and original;
but the part that is good is not original,
and the part that is original is not good.

DR SAMUEL JOHNSON (1709–1784)
English author and lexicographer

ও Dublin University contains the cream of
Ireland – rich and thick.

SAMUEL BECKETT (1906–1989)
Irish dramatist – using 'thick' for 'stupid'

❧ The problem with Ireland is that it's a country full of genius, but with absolutely no talent.

HUGH LEONARD

❧ The Irish people do not gladly suffer common sense.

OLIVER ST JOHN GOGARTY (1878–1957)
Irish writer

❧ You may have genius. The contrary is, of course, probable.

OLIVER WENDELL HOLMES (1809–1894)
American writer

❧ I have found some of the best reasons for remaining at the bottom simply by looking at the men at the top.

FRANK MORE COLBY

❧ A bore is a man who, when you ask him how he is, he tells you.

BERT LESTON TAYLOR (1866–1939)
American poet

❧ You've got the brain of a four-year-old boy, and I bet he was glad to get rid of it.

GROUCHO MARX (1890–1977)
American comic actor

❧ He had been kicked in the head by a mule
when young and believed everything he
read in the Sunday papers.

GEORGE ADE (1866–1944)

❧ Blessed is the man who, having nothing to
say, abstains from giving wordy evidence
of the fact.

GEORGE ELIOT (1819–1880)
English novelist

❧ He is so mean, he won't let his little baby
have more than one measle at a time.

EUGENE FIELD (1850–1895)
American critic

❧ He is so mean that he would not give you a drip from the end of his nose.

ANONYMOUS TRADITIONAL

❧ Cambridge people rarely smile,
Being urban, squat and packed with
guile . . .

RUPERT BROOKE (1887–1915)
English poet

❧ Never trust a man with short legs – brains too near the bottom

NOËL COWARD (1899–1973)
English actor and playwright

❧ A very ugly man. He has moreover a thin, flat behind which implies shallowness of character.

JAMES LEES-MILNE (1908–1997)
English writer, on Noël Coward

❧ He hasn't the brains of a bandicoot.

AUSTRALIAN SLANG INSULT

❧ I've never any pity for conceited people because I think they carry their comfort around with them.

GEORGE ELIOT (1819–1880)

❧ Civilized men arrived in the Pacific armed
with alcohol, syphilis, trousers and the
Bible.

HAVELOCK ELLIS (1859–1939)
English writer

❧ He was distinguished for ignorance; for he
had only one idea and that was wrong.

BENJAMIN DISRAELI (1804–1881)
British prime minister

☘ There are two kinds of fools: one says, 'This is old, therefore it is good'; the other says , 'this is new, therefore it is better.'

REVEREND WILLIAM INGE (1860–1954)
English divine

☘ Some men are graduated from college *cum laude*, some are graduated *summa cum laude*, and some are graduated *mirabile dictu*.

WILLIAM TAFT (1857–1930)
American president

❧ I do not tolerate bores well. A bore is a man who deprives you of solitude without providing you with company.

GIAN VICENZA GRAVINA
Italian author of the eighteenth century

❧ Sir Stafford has a brilliant mind until it is made up.

MARGOT ASQUITH (1864–1945)
prime-ministerial wife, on Sir Stafford Cripps

❧ Rosalind Russell . . . one of those few film stars who can read without her lips moving.

LEONARD MOSLEY
Daily Express

❦ He is the only genius with an IQ of 60.

GORE VIDAL (1927–)
American author, on Andy Warhol

❦ The bubonic plagiarist.

DR JONATHAN MILLER (1934–)
English polymath, on David Frost

❦ It's lucky for you that you have a hole in the end of your penis. Otherwise, oxygen couldn't get to your brain.

ANONYMOUS

❧ My vibrator is bigger than that, and it has a higher IQ too.

ANONYMOUS
an anatomical comment

❧ The man who reads nothing at all is better educated than the man who reads nothing but newspapers.

THOMAS JEFFERSON (1743–1826)
American president

❧ It is better to be silent and be thought a fool than to speak and remove all doubt.

MARK TWAIN (1835–1910)
American writer

❧ The greatest mind ever to stay in prep
school.

NORMAN MAILER (1923–)
American writer, on J. D. Salinger

❧ A kangaroo loose in the top paddock.

TRADITIONAL AUSTRALIAN SLANG

❧ His ignorance is encyclopaedic.

ABBA EBAN (1915–2002)
Israeli diplomat

❧ He is a few kopeks short of a ruble . . .

TRADITIONAL RUSSIAN INSULT

❧ He knows so little – and knows it so fluently.

ELLEN GLASGOW (1874–1945)
American writer

❧ No self-respecting fish would be wrapped in a Murdoch newspaper.

MIKE ROYKO

❧ She's afraid she'll void her warranty if she thinks too much.

ANONYMOUS

∞ Noël Coward was once informed that a rather boorish and not intellectually dazzling acquaintance had blown his brains out. Spontaneously Coward said: 'He must have been an incredibly good shot.'

∞ He rose without a trace.

KITTY MUGGERIDGE
on David Frost

∞ He is a mental midget with the IQ of a fence-post.

TOM WAITS (1949–)
Musician

He has a 10k brain attached to a
30 gigabyte mouth.

ANONYMOUS
said of an I. T. consultant

It's great to be with Bill Buckley because
you don't have to think. He takes a
position and you automatically take the
opposite, and you know you are right.

J. K. GALBRAITH (1908–)
Canadian economist

He doesn't know the meaning of the word 'fear'. Of course, there are lots of words he doesn't know the meaning of.

SID GILMAN
American football coach

Yeah, I'd love to fuck your brains out, but apparently someone beat me to it.

ANONYMOUS

❧ If it squirms, it's biology; if it stinks, it's chemistry; if it doesn't work, it's physics and if you can't understand it, it's mathematics.

MAGNUS PYKE
eccentric English scientist and TV presenter

❧ 'The best confidential report I ever hear of,' said Lord Wavell, 'was also the shortest. It was by one Horse Gunner of another, and ran: 'Personally I would not breed from this officer.'

MAJOR-GENERAL R. J. COLLINS
in Lord Wavell

❧ He has a photographic memory.
Unfortunately the lens cap is glued on.

ANONYMOUS

❧ The 'g' is silent – unfortunately the only part
of her that is.

JULIE BURCHILL
English journalist, on Camille Paglia

❧ You have a half-horsepower brain, pulling
a two-ton mouth.

ANONYMOUS
*to Richard Meltzer on the latter's article
about Paul McCartney*

❧ I phoned my local cab firm and said: 'Can you please send me a big, fat racist bastard with a personal hygiene problem some time before I have my menopause?'

JO BRAND
English comedienne

❧ He has a 3.5-inch drive, but his data on punch cards.

ANONYMOUS COMPUTER BUFF

❧ A room temperature IQ . . .

ANONYMOUS

ᴥ His brain is as full of shit as a
Christmas goose.

ANONYMOUS

ᴥ An acquaintance: a degree of friendship
called slight when the object is poor or
obscure, and intimate when he is rich
or famous.

And

A cynic: a blackguard who sees things as
they are, and not as they ought to be.

AMBROSE BIERCE (1842–1914)
American writer and journalist

❧ There is no opinion so absurd but that some philosopher will express it.

MARCUS TULLIUS CICERO (106–43 BC)

❧ A twonk, a twit, a decorticated turnip on a dull day, a vacant house, a cerebral basement with no upper floor, a deep-fried dog's bollock, a man in whose head all the lacunae are holding hands, a mental void, a slack-jawed empty-eyed tabloid-reading slacker, a telly vegetable, a spreading-arsed numb-nuts couch potato with a mind stuck in neutral and the IQ of a bread-stick . . .

ASSORTED ANONYMOUS ASSAULTS

Politics – insult's fountainhead

❦ A politician is an animal who can sit on the fence and keep both ears to the ground.

H. L. MENCKEN (1880–1956)
American editor and writer

❦ A pig, an ass, a dunghill, the spawn of an adder, a basilisk, a lying buffoon, a mad fool with a frothy mouth . . . a lubberly ass . . . a frantic madman.

MARTIN LUTHER (1483–1546)
German religious reformer, on Henry VIII

❦ Spongy eyes, and a supple conscience . . .

COLONEL EDWARD SAXBY
on Oliver Cromwell

❧ Every time I fill a vacant office, I make ten
malcontents and one ingrate.

LOUIS XIV OF FRANCE (1638–1715)

❧ His crimes are the only great thing
about him.

RICHARD BRINSLEY SHERIDAN (1751–1816)
Irish dramatist, on Warren Hastings

❧ I tremble for my country when I reflect
that God is just.

THOMAS JEFFERSON (1743–1826)
American president

❧ That dark designing sordid ambitious vain proud arrogant and vindictive knave.

GENERAL CHARLES LEE (1731–1782)
American general, on George Washington

❧ Treacherous in private friendship and a hypocrite in public life, the world will be puzzled to decide whether you are an apostate or an imposter, whether you have abandoned good principles, or whether you ever had any?

TOM PAINE (1737–1809)
English radical, on George Washington

 ☞ George the Third
Ought never to have occurred
One can only wonder
At so grotesque a blunder.

E. CLERIHEW BENTLEY (1875–1956)

English journalist and poet

☞ The great parliamentarian, John Wilkes, was
once heckled by a potential voter who said
that he would rather vote for the devil than
for Wilkes. The quick-witted Wilkes replied
without hesitation:

'And if your friend is not standing . . . ?'

TOM SHERIDAN: I think, father, that many men who are called great patriots in the House of Commons are really great humbugs. For my own part, when I get into Parliament, I will pledge myself to no party, but write upon my forehead in legible characters, 'To Be Let'.

RICHARD BRINSLEY SHERIDAN: And under it, Tom, write 'Unfurnished'.

RICHARD BRINSLEY SHERIDAN (1751–1816)
Irish dramatist

❧ LORD CHATHAM: If I cannot speak standing,
I will speak sitting; and if I cannot speak
sitting I will speak lying.
LORD NORTH: Which he will do in whatever
position he speaks.

❧ How Thomas Paine gets a living now, or
what brothel he inhabits I know not . . .
Like Judas he will be remembered by
posterity; men will learn to express all that
is base, malignant, treacherous, unnatural
and blasphemous by the single
monosyllable – Paine.

WILLIAM COBBETT (1762–1835)
English essayist and politician

❧ I have no small talk and Peel has
no manners.

ARTHUR WELLESLEY,
DUKE OF WELLINGTON (1769–1852)
British prime minister, on Sir Robert Peel

❧ Nouns of number, or multitude, such as
Mob, Parliament, Rabble, House of
Commons, Regiment, Court of King's
Bench, Den of Thieves, and the like.

WILLIAM COBBETT (1762–1835)
English Grammar,
Syntax as Relating to Pronouns

⚬ He was a man of splendid abilities but utterly corrupt. Like rotten mackerel by moonlight, he shines and stinks.

JOHN RANDOLPH (1773–1833)
*Representative for Roanoak, Virginia,
on Edward Livingstone*

⚬ What will now be said to this cowardly crowing of pompous chanticleer upon his own dunghill?

WILLIAM COBBETT (1762–1835)
on Henry Addington, Viscount Sidmouth

❧ The president is nothing more than a well-meaning baboon . . . I went to the White House directly after tea where I found the original gorilla about as intelligent as ever. What a specimen to be the head of our affairs now!

GEORGE MCCLELLEN (1826–1885)
American general, on Abraham Lincoln

❧ He can compress the most words into the smallest idea of any man I ever met.

ABRAHAM LINCOLN (1809–1865)
American president, on one of his political enemies

❧ If a traveller were informed that such a man was the leader of the House of Commons, he might begin to comprehend how the Egyptians worshipped an insect.

BENJAMIN DISRAELI (1804–1881)
British prime minister, on Lord John Russell

❧ Mr Depew says that if you open my mouth and drop in a dinner, up will come a speech. But I warn you that if you open your mouths and drop in one of Mr Depew's speeches, up will come your dinners.

JOSEPH H. CHOATE (1832–1917)
politician, on Senator Chauncey Depew

ॐ We did not conceive it possible that even
Mr Lincoln would produce a paper so
slipshod, so loose-joined, so puerile, not
alone in its literary construction, but in its
ideas, its sentiments, its grasp. He has
outdone himself. He has literally come out
of the little end of his own horn. By the side
of it, mediocrity is superb.

CHICAGO TIMES, 1863
on Abraham Lincoln's Gettysburg Address

ॐ Reader, suppose you were an idiot; and
suppose you were a member of Congress;
but I repeat myself . . .

MARK TWAIN (1835–1910)
American writer

❧ The most extraordinary collection of sturdy beggars, parsons, priests, pensioners, army people, navy people, place-men, bank directors, and stock and land jobbers ever established to act as a paltry screen to a rotten government.

WILLIAM LYON MACKENZIE
on the Canadian Legislative Council

❧ A politician is a person with whose politics you do not agree: if you agree with him he is a statesman.

DAVID LLOYD GEORGE (1863–1945)
British prime minister

❧ He had a bungalow mind.

WOODROW WILSON (1856–1924)
American president, on Warren G. Harding

❧ I have no trouble with my enemies. But my goddam friends . . . they are the ones that keep me walking the floor nights.

WARREN G. HARDING (1865–1923)
American president

❧ They never open their mouths without subtracting from the sum of human knowledge.

THOMAS REED
on members of Congress

❧ He was simply a hole in the air.

GEORGE ORWELL (1903–1950)
*English novelist and essayist,
on Stanley Baldwin*

❧ Enough to make a civil servant turn in his groove.

COLLIE KNOX

❧ He is like trying to pick up mercury with a fork.

DAVID LLOYD GEORGE (1863–1945)
on negotiations with Eamon de Valera

✌ Like a cushion, he always bore the impress
of the last man who sat upon him.

DAVID LLOYD GEORGE (1863–1945)
on Lord Derby

✌ All the extraordinary men I have ever
known were chiefly extraordinary in their
own estimation.

WOODROW WILSON (1856–1924)

✌ When they circumcised Herbert Samuel
they threw away the wrong bit.

DAVID LLOYD GEORGE (1863–1945)

❧ A chameleon on plaid.

HERBERT HOOVER (1874–1964)
American president, on Franklin D. Roosevelt

❧ A glass of port in his hand and a fat cigar in his mouth, with a huge and bloody red steak which he puts in his mouth in big chunks, and chews and chatters . . . until the blood trickles down his chin – and to think this monster comes of a good family.

JOSEPH GOEBBELS (1897–1945)
*German Minister of Public Enlightenment,
depicting Winston Churchill in the
House of Commons*

❧ To err is Truman.

WALTER WINCHELL

❧ He reminds me of nothing so much as a
dead fish before it has had time to stiffen.

GEORGE ORWELL (1903–1950)
on Clement Attlee

❧ The only good government is a bad one
in a hell of a fright.

JOYCE CARY
The Horse's Mouth

ა There's no point in voting. Whoever you
vote for, you get the government . . .

TRADITIONAL IRISH SAYING

ა Underground we have coal for 600 years.
Above it we have Mr Shinwell. Reversal
of these positions would solve our present
troubles.

R. A. WHITSUN
in the Yorkshire Post

‣ In Russia a man is called reactionary if he objects to having his property stolen and his wife and children murdered.

> WINSTON CHURCHILL (1874–1965)
> *British prime minister*

‣ HERBERT MORRISON: I don't know what is the matter with the opposition today.
WINSTON CHURCHILL: You should look in a looking-glass.

∞ MR GAMMONS: Do you realise that more gin might help the people of London to forget the Labour Government?

MINISTER OF FOOD: Much more gin would be necessary to make them forget the previous Government.

HANSARD

∞ NANCY ASTOR TO WINSTON CHURCHILL: Winston, if you were my husband, I'd put poison in my coffee.

CHURCHILL: Madam, if you were my wife I'd drink it.

❧ BESSIE BRADDOCK MP TO WINSTON CHURCHILL:
Winston, if that belly were on a woman,
she'd be pregnant.
CHURCHILL: Madam, it has been – and she is.

❧ Pathological exhibits . . . paranoiacs,
degenerates, morons, bludgers . . . pack of
dingoes . . . industrial outlaws and political
lepers . . . ratbags. If these people went to
Russia, Stalin wouldn't even use them for
manure.

MR CALWELL
Minister of Immigration and Information on
communists among his fellow Australians

❦ He can lie out of both sides of his mouth
at the same time, and even if he found
himself telling the truth, he'd lie to keep
his hand in.

HARRY S. TRUMAN (1884–1972)
American president, on Richard Nixon

❦ He has the lucidity which is the by-product
of a fundamentally sterile mind . . .
Listening to a speech by Chamberlain is like
paying a visit to Woolworths; everything in
its place and nothing above sixpence.

ANEURIN BEVAN (1897–1960)
British politician, on Neville Chamberlain

೫ Nixon is a purposeless man, but I have great faith in his cowardice.

JIMMY BRESLIN (1930–)
American Pulitzer Prize journalist

೫ Q: How can you tell when he's lying?
   A: When his lips are moving.

BBC TV'S *That Was The Week That Was
on Harold Wilson*

೫ It is not enough to have every intelligent person in the country voting for me – I need a majority.

ADLAI STEVENSON (1900–1965)
American politician

❧ I always wanted to get into politics, but I was never light enough to get in the team.

ART BUCHWALD (1925–)
American columnist

❧ An editor is one who separates the wheat from the chaff, and prints the chaff.

ADLAI STEVENSON (1900–1965)

❧ Your public servants serve you right; indeed they often serve you better than your apathy and indifference deserve.

ADLAI STEVENSON (1900–1965)

❧ Anyone with an appetite for politics should be barred from office by that very reason.

ANONYMOUS

❧ Every time Mr Macmillan comes back from abroad Mr Butler goes to the airport and grips him warmly by the throat.

HAROLD WILSON
British prime minister, describing Harold
Macmillan and R. A. B. Butler

❧ A politician is an arse upon which everyone has say except a man.

e. e. cummings (1894–1962)
American writer, 'A Politician'

❧ Anyone who extends the right hand of fellowship is in danger of losing a couple of fingers.

ALVA JOHNSON
on Mayor La Guardia of New York

❧ It is now known that men enter local politics solely as a result of being unhappily married.

G. NORTHCOTE PARKINSON
Parkinson's Law

Ω Being attacked by the Right Honourable Gentleman is like being savaged by a dead sheep.

DENIS HEALEY (1917–)
*British politician, on criticism from
Sir Geoffrey Howe*

Ω The government has been faced with an orchestrated campaign of pressures from newspapers. They even had the gargantuan intellect of Bernard Levin squeaking away in the undergrowth like a demented vole.

DENNIS HEALEY (1917–)

❧ If God had been a Liberal, there wouldn't have been ten commandments, there would have been ten suggestions.

MALCOLM BRADBURY AND CHRISTOPHER BIGSBY
After Dinner Game

❧ Ronald Reagan is a triumph of the embalmer's art.

GORE VIDAL (1927–)
American author

❧ Gerry Ford is so dumb he can't fart and chew gum at the same time.

LYNDON BAINES JOHNSON (1908–1973)
American president, on Gerald Ford

❧ Gerry Ford is a nice guy, but he played too much football with his helmet off.

LYNDON BAINES JOHNSON (1908–1973)

❧ Dr Rhodes Boyson might also clamber back into his Cruickshank engraving and return to whatever unpublished Dickens novel he appears in.

SIMON HOGGART (1949–)
English journalist

❧ Liberal: Someone who believes crime is the fault of Society – until he's robbed.

JERRY TUCKER

❧ He looks like the guy in a science fiction
movie who is the first to see the Creature.

DAVID FRYE
on Gerald Ford

❧ Congressmen are so damned dumb they
could throw themselves at the ground –
and miss.

JAMES TRAFICANT (1941–)
politician

❧ It is inexcusable for scientists to torture
animals; let them make their experiments
on journalists and politicians.

HENRIK IBSEN (1828–1906)
Norwegian dramatist

Xenophobia rules

∞ A Canadian is someone who drinks
Brazilian coffee from an English teacup,
and munches a French pastry while sitting
on his Danish furniture, having just come
from an Italian movie in his German car.
He picks up his Japanese pen and writes
to his Member of Parliament to complain
about the American takeover of the
Canadian publishing business.

CAMPBELL HUGHES

∞ Quebec does not have opinions – only
sentiments.

SIR WILFRID LAURIER (1841–1919)
English politician

❧ How utterly destitute of all light and charm
are the intellectual conditions of our people
and the institutions of our public life! How
barren! How barbarous!

> ARCHIBALD LAMPMAN (1861–1899)
> *Canadian poet*

❧ The purity of the air of Newfoundland is
without doubt due to the fact that the
people of the outports never open their
windows.

> J. G. MILLAIS
> *(reported in 1907)*

❧ Quebec is not a province like the others.
   She is a little more stupid.

GERARD FILION

❧ England, the heart of a rabbit in the body of
   a lion,
   The jaws of a serpent, in an abode of
   popinjays.

EUGENE DESCHAMPS
on fourteenth-century England

❧ The Welsh are so damn Welsh that it looks
   like affectation.

PROFESSOR WALTER RALEIGH (1861–1922)
English scholar

∽ There is constant activity going on in one small portion of the brain; all the rest is stagnant. The money-making faculty is alone cultivated. They are incapable of acquiring general knowledge on a broad or liberal scale. All is confined to trade, finance, law and small, local, provincial matters. Art, science, literature, are nearly dead letters to them.

T. C. GRATTAN (1792–1864)
on nineteenth-century America

∽ The Irish are a fair people: they never speak well of each other.

DR SAMUEL JOHNSON (1709–1784)
English author and lexicographer

In the four corners of the globe, who reads an American book? Or goes to an American play? Or looks at an American picture or statue? What does the world yet owe to American physicians or surgeons? . . . Who drinks out of American glasses? Or eats from American plates? Or wears American coats or gowns? Or sleeps in American blankets? Finally, under which of the old tyrannical governments of Europe is every sixth man a slave, whom his fellow creatures may buy and sell and torture?

SYDNEY SMITH (1771–1845)
English clergyman and essayist

❧ I showed my appreciation of my native land in the usual Irish way; by getting out of it as soon as I possibly could.

GEORGE BERNARD SHAW (1856–1950)
Anglo-Irish dramatist

❧ No one who has any self-respect stays in Ireland, but flees afar as though from a country that has undergone the visitation of an angered Jove.

JAMES JOYCE (1882–1941)
Irish writer

❧ What is an Aussie's idea of foreplay?
'Brace yourself, Sheila.'
and
How do you make an Aussie laugh on
Monday?
Tell him a joke on Friday . . .
and
What do you call an Aussie with half a brain?
Gifted.

ANONYMOUS

❧ Much may be made of a Scotsman, if he
be caught young.

DR SAMUEL JOHNSON (1709–1784)

❧ That garret of the earth – the knuckle-end of England – that land of Calvin, oat-cakes and sulphur.

SYDNEY SMITH (1771–1845)
on Scotland

❧ Have you heard about the Scot who took a taxi to the bankruptcy court? When he arrived, he asked the driver in as one of his creditors.

SCOTTISH JOKE

&c After hours of painstaking microsurgery, and
with 107 tiny stitches around his wrist, Ali
Al-Dazid was recovering in hospital when he
was visited by a friend.
'I see you won your appeal then, Ali,' said
his visitor.

&c A traditional Scottish recipe starts 'first
borrow four eggs . . .'

&c What do you call an Iranian who practises
birth control?
A humanitarian.

✎ [Britain] . . . a soggy little island, always huffing and puffing to keep up with Western Europe.

JOHN UPDIKE (1932–)
American novelist

✎ The average cooking in the average hotel for the average Englishman explains to a large extent the English bleakness and taciturnity. Nobody can beam and warble while chewing pressed beef smeared with diabolical mustard. Nobody can exult aloud while ungluing from his teeth a quivering tapioca pudding.

KAREL CAPEK (1890–1938)

❧ Let the eastern bastards freeze in the dark.

BUMPER STICKER OF 1973, ALBERTA

❧ When I first saw the [Niagara] falls I was disappointed . . . Every American bride is taken there, and the sight must be one of the earliest, if not the keenest, disappointments of American married life.

OSCAR WILDE (1856–1900)
British dramatist and poet

❧ British Columbia is a barren, cold, mountain country that is not worth keeping . . . the place has been going from bad to worse. Fifty railroads would not galvanise it into prosperity.

HENRY LABOUCHÈRE

❧ Toronto as a city carries out the idea of Canada as a country. It is a calculated crime both against the aspirations of the soul and the affection of the heart.

ALEISTER CROWLEY

I do not dislike the French from the vulgar antipathy between neighbouring nations, but for their insolent and unfounded air of superiority.

HORACE WALPOLE (1717–1797)
English writer

France was long a despotism tempered by epigrams.

THOMAS CARLYLE (1795–1881)
Scottish historian

co The French are sawed-off sissies who eat
snails and slugs and cheese that smells like
people's feet. Utter cowards who force their
own children to drink wine, they gibber like
baboons even when you try to speak to
them in their own wimpy language.

P. J. O'ROURKE (1947–)
American writer and satirist

co Paris is like a whore, from a distance she
seems ravishing, you can't wait until you
have her in your arms. Five minutes later,
you feel empty, disgusted with yourself.
You feel tricked.

HENRY MILLER (1891–1980)
American writer

ℚ Having to go to war without France is sort of like having to go deer hunting without an accordion.

ROSS PEROT
American presidential candidate

ℚ I assumed the French would be capable of going with us to Iraq so they could be there to instruct the Iraqis on how to surrender.

PETER KING

꙰ A Russian lay dying on his squalid bed when
   there was a thunderous knock on the door.
     'Who is it?' he croaked.
     'The Angel of Death,' a voice grated.
     'Thank God,' gasped the Russian,
   'I thought it was the KGB.'

ANONYMOUS TRADITIONAL

꙰ Why is it that in New Zealand you can
   never find a Kiwi [a New Zealander]
   who can swim?
   Simple. If they *can* swim, they're all in
   Australia.

ANONYMOUS

∾ There are only two kinds of Chinese – those who give bribes and those who take them.

RUSSIAN PROVERB

∾ A fighting Frenchman runs away from even a she goat.

RUSSIAN PROVERB

∾ Why are rectal thermometers banned in Italy?
It was found that they did too much brain damage.

ANONYMOUS

✕ California is a fine place to live – if you happen to be an orange.

FRED ALLEN (1894–1956)
American radio comedian

✕ There was a German so ignorant that he thought Einstein was a glass of beer.

ANONYMOUS

✕ The reason there is so little crime in Germany is that it's against the law.

ALEX LEVIN

❧ The German may be a good fellow, but it is best to hang him all the same.

RUSSIAN SAYING

❧ I speak Spanish to God, Italian to women, French to men, and German to my horse.

EMPEROR CHARLES V (1500–1558)

❧ German is a language which was developed solely to afford the speaker the opportunity to spit at strangers under the guise of polite conversation.

NATIONAL LAMPOON

ॐ Because of their cuisine, Germans don't consider farting rude. They'd certainly be out of luck if they did.

P. J. O'ROURKE (1947–)
American writer and satirist

ॐ The great virtues of the German people have created more vices than idleness did . . .

PAUL VALÉRY (1871–1945)
French poet

ॐ Germany, the diseased world's bathhouse.

MARK TWAIN (1835–1910)
American writer

❧ How much disgruntled heaviness,
lameness, dampness, how much beer is
the German intelligence.

FRIEDRICH NIETZSCHE (1844–1900)
German philosopher

❧ The East German manages to combine a
Teutonic capacity for bureaucracy with a
Russian capacity for infinite delay.

GORONWY REES (1909–1979)
Welsh writer and journalist

❧ His great aim was to escape from
civilization, and as soon as he had money,
he went to Southern California.

ANONYMOUS

❧ America is one long expectoration.

OSCAR WILDE (1856–1900)

❧ It was wonderful to find America, but it
would have been more wonderful to miss it.

MARK TWAIN (1835–1910)
American writer

∞ Of course, America had often been
discovered before Columbus, but it had
always been hushed up.

OSCAR WILDE (1856–1900)

∞ Don't get the idea that I'm one of these
goddam radicals. Don't get the idea that I'm
knocking the American system.

AL CAPONE (1899–1947)
American gangster

❧ In America law and custom alike are based upon the dreams of spinsters.

BERTRAND RUSSELL (1873–1970)
British philosopher

❧ What a pity we have no amusements in England but vice and religion.

SYDNEY SMITH (1771–1845)

❧ Why is English beer so like making love in a canoe?
Because they are both fucking close to water.

AUSTRALIAN GRAFFITO

❧ A pirate spreading misery and ruin over
the face of the ocean.

THOMAS JEFFERSON (1743–1826)
American president, describing the British

❧ I know why the sun never sets on the
British Empire: God wouldn't trust
an Englishman in the dark.

DUNCAN SPAETH (1868–1954)
American academic

❧ On a visit to London, Mahatma Gandhi was asked what he thought of Western civilization. 'I think it would be a good idea,' he said.

❧ Paralytic sycophants, effete betrayers of humanity, carrion-eating servile imitators, arch-cowards and collaborators, gang of women-murderers, degenerate rabble, parasitic traditionalists, play-boy soldiers, conceited dandies.

Descriptions of the British approved for use by the East German Communist party

❧ German is the most extravagantly ugly
language – it sounds like someone using a
sick bag on a 747.

WILLY RUSHTON
English satirist

❧ In America only the successful writer
is important, in France all writers are
important, in England no writer is
important, and in Australia you have
to explain what a writer is.

GEOFFREY COTTRELL

❧ In Australia, not reading poetry is the
national pastime.

PHYLLIS MCGINLEY

❧ I find it hard to say if I liked the place; when
I was there, it appeared to be shut.

CLEMENT FREUD (1924–)
writer and politician, on Australia

❧ Australia may be the only country in the
world in which the term 'Academic' is
regularly used as a term of abuse.

DAME LEONIE KRAMER

∞ The Americans, like the English, probably make love worse than any other race.

WALT WHITMAN (1819–1892)
American poet

∞ Their demeanour . . . is invariably morose, sullen, clownish, and repulsive. I should think there is not, on the face of the earth, a people so entirely destitute of humour, vivacity, or the capacity for enjoyment.

CHARLES DICKENS (1812–1870)
English novelist, on the Americans

  If I owned Texas and Hell, I would rent
  out Texas and live in Hell.

PHILIP H. SHERIDAN (1831–1888)
American general

  America is the only nation in history which
  miraculously has gone directly from
  barbarism to degeneration without the usual
  interval of civilisation.

GEORGES CLEMENCEAU (1841–1929)
French president

∓ I wonder if nature intended for me to be
an American rather than an Englishman.
I think I should make a better American,
yet I hold it higher to be a bad Englishman
than a good American.

ANTHONY TROLLOPE (1815–1882)
English novelist

∓ The 100% American is 99% an idiot.

GEORGE BERNARD SHAW (1856–1950)
Anglo-Irish dramatist

❧ Trollope has a gross and repulsive face and manner, but appears *bon enfant* when you talk with him. But he is the dullest Briton of them all.

HENRY JAMES (1843–1916)
American novelist

❧ No one ever went broke underestimating the taste of the American public.

H. L. MENCKEN (1880–1956)
American editor and writer

❧ Cross yourself once before an Andalusian and thrice on spotting an Italian.

SPANISH SAYING

If there is a Hell, Rome is built on top of it.

GERMAN SAYING

Rome reminds me of a man who lives by exhibiting to travellers his grandmother's corpse.

JAMES JOYCE (1882–1941)
Irish writer

The Japanese have almost as big a reputation for cruelty as do young children.

DENNIS BLOODWORTH

છ Poland is now a totally independent nation, and it has managed to greatly improve its lifestyle thanks to the introduction of modern Western conveniences such as food.

DAVE BARRY (1947–)
American writer and journalist

છ The French don't care what they do as long as they pronounce it properly.

GEORGE BERNARD SHAW (1856–1950)
Anglo-Irish dramatist

❧ The English instinctively admire any man
who has no talent and is modest about it.

JAMES AGATE (1877–1947)
English dramatic critic

❧ He lies like a French bulletin.

TRADITIONAL DUTCH SAYING

❧ An Englishman will burn his bed to
catch a flea.

TURKISH PROVERB

❦ It must be acknowledged that the English
   are the most disagreeable of all the nations
   of Europe – more surly and morose, with
   less disposition to please, to exert
   themselves for the good of society, to make
   small sacrifices, and to put themselves out
   of their way.

SYDNEY SMITH (1771–1845)

❦ On a fine day the climate of England is like
   looking up a chimney; on a foul day, like
   looking down one.

ANONYMOUS

❧ The English think that incompetence [in sex] is the same thing as sincerity.

QUENTIN CRISP
English wit and dramatic performer

❧ Poms don't have much imagination because they've pinched most of their street names off the Monopoly board.

PAUL HOGAN
Australian actor

❧ The German mind has a talent for making no mistakes but the very greatest.

CLIFTON FADIMAN (1904–1999)
American author and editor

❧ A German singer! I would as soon get
  pleasure from the neighing of my horse.

FREDERICK THE GREAT OF PRUSSIA (1712–1786)

❧ Greeks tell the truth, but only once a year.

RUSSIAN PROVERB

❧ Norway – the sun never sets, the bar never
  opens, and the whole country smells of
  kippers.

EVELYN WAUGH (1903–1966)
English novelist

ॐ Belgium is a country invented by the British to annoy the French.

CHARLES DE GAULLE (1890–1970)
French president

ॐ If one could teach the English to talk and the Irish to listen, society would be quite civilized.

OSCAR WILDE (1856–1900)

⊛ You must not miss Whitehall. At one end you will find a statue of one of our kings who was beheaded; at the other, the monument of the man who did it. This is just an example of our attempts to be fair to everybody.

SIR EDWARD APPLETON

⊛ My one claim to originality among Irishmen is that I have never made a speech.

GEORGE MOORE (1852–1933)
Irish writer

❧ An Irishman can be worried by the consciousness that there is nothing to worry about.

AUSTIN O'MALLEY (1858 –1932)

❧ The Irish do not want anyone to wish them well; they want everyone to wish their enemies ill.

HAROLD NICHOLSON (1886–1968)
British diplomat and writer

❧ [The Irish] is one race of people for whom psychoanalysis is of no use whatsoever.

SIGMUND FREUD (1856–1939)
Austrian founder of psychoanalysis

∝ Other people have a nationality. The Irish and the Jews have a psychosis.

BRENDAN BEHAN (1923–1964)
Irish writer

∝ An Irish farmer, to cover the possibility of unexpected visitors, can often be found eating his dinner out of a drawer.

NIALL TOIBIN (1929–)
Irish actor

∝ The old sow who always eats her young.

JAMES JOYCE (1882–1941)
on Ireland

❧ The Japanese have perfected good manners and made them indistinguishable from rudeness.

PAUL THEROUX (1941–)
American travel writer

❧ . . . a nation of sheep. Angry sheep, but nevertheless sheep, and in sheep's clothing.

JAMES KIRKUP (1918–)
English poet and translator, on Russians

∾ Russians will consume marinated
mushrooms and vodka, salted herring
and vodka, smoked salmon and vodka,
salami and vodka, caviar on brown bread
and vodka, pickled cucumbers and vodka,
cold tongue and vodka, red beet salad and
vodka, scallions and vodka – anything and
everything and vodka.

HEDRICK SMITH (1933–)
American journalist and writer

∾ How can you tell a Russian? Go to sleep
and he will rob you.

UKRAINIAN SAYING

∞ Q: Did you hear about the man who was
half Italian and half Polish?
A: He made himself an offer he couldn't
understand.

ANONYMOUS

∞ Heaven for climate, Hell for society.

MARK TWAIN (1835–1910)
American writer

∞ It takes a surgical operation to get a joke
well into a Scotsman's understanding.

SYDNEY SMITH (1771–1845)

ॐ The kilt is an unrivalled garment for fornication and diarrhoea.

JOHN MASTERS
on Scotland

ॐ The great thing about Glasgow is that if there is a nuclear attack, it'll look exactly the same afterwards.

BILLY CONNOLLY
Scottish comedian

ॐ Nationalism is a silly cock crowing on its own dunghill.

RICHARD ALDINGTON (1892–1962)
English novelist and biographer

Royal remarks and foot/mouth interfaces

❧ My brother, John, is not the man to conquer a country if there is anyone to offer even the feeblest resistance.

RICHARD I, THE LIONHEART (1157–1199)
on his brother, who attempted to take the throne
while Richard was on a crusade

❧ Heart, liver and lungs and all the interior of the said William out of which such perverse thoughts had proceeded, to be thrown into the fire and burnt.

EDWARD I (1239–1307)
ordering William Wallace, the leader of the Scots,
to be disembowelled

The king of France, is he as tall as I am? Is he stout? What sort of leg has he? He is indeed a worthy and honest sovereign, but he is nevertheless a Frenchman and not to be trusted.

HENRY VIII (1491–1547)
on Francis I

A venomous serpent, an infernal wolf . . . detestable trumpeter of pride, calumnies and schism.

HENRY VIII (1491–1547)
on Martin Luther

❧ This day a man died with much wit and
   very little judgement.

ELIZABETH I (1533–1603)
as Princess Elizabeth, then fifteen, on the
execution of her guardian, Admiral Seymour

❧ [The Church of England] . . . is the middle
   way between the pomp of superstitious
   tyranny and the meanness of fantastic
   anarchy.

CHARLES II (1630–1685)

❧ Odd's fish. They are all dull and foggy.

CHARLES II (1630–1685)
*on the German princesses
suggested to him as possible brides*

❧ I think of him so ugly that I am obliged to
turn my head away in disgust when he is
speaking to me. Marry I will, and that
directly to enjoy my liberty, but not the
Prince of Orange.

PRINCESS CHARLOTTE, DAUGHTER OF GEORGE III
on hearing her father's choice of husband for her

෮ Always scribble, scribble, scribble. Another damned, thick, square book, eh, Mr Gibbon?

THE DUKE OF GLOUCESTER,
BROTHER TO GEORGE III
when presented with the latest volume of Gibbon's Decline and Fall of the Roman Empire

෮ Oh, bugger Bognor!

GEORGE V (1865–1936)
on being told he should go there to recuperate from an illness

ⅆ . . . sadistic and incompetent.

GEORGE VI (1895–1952)
on a short-stayed nanny

ⅆ He looks like a small, quiet man with a feeble voice, but he is really a tyrant. He was quite polite.

GEORGE VI
on V. M. Molotov, Soviet Foreign Minister

ⅆ It looks like a tart's bedroom.

PRINCE PHILIP, DUKE OF EDINBURGH (1921–)
on the Duchess of York's interior decoration

❧ I don't think so. Unless it farts and eats
grass she's not interested.

PRINCE PHILIP
*on being asked if the Queen would like to look at
the flight deck of Concorde*

❧ Ah, I see the pubs have just closed . . .

PRINCE PHILIP
*observing the late arrival of the Press
during a tour of Australia.*

❧ What Philip calls one silly mug
put on another.

QUEEN ELIZABETH II (1926–)
*on the Jubilee mugs produced for
her Silver Jubilee in 1977*

❧ A bloody awful newspaper. It is full of lies, scandal and imagination. It is a vicious newspaper.

PRINCE PHILIP
on the Daily Express

❧ I declare this thing open – whatever it is.

PRINCE PHILIP
having a memory lapse during ceremonial duties in Canada. In his honour the East Annexe of Vancouver Town Hall is now known as the East Thing.

Snappish one-liners and bruising retorts

❧ She's not what she was fifteen years ago –
she's eight years older.

❧ If I've said anything to insult you – believe
me, I've tried my utmost.

❧ Prevent air pollution – for all our sakes, stop
talking.

❧ Have I met you somewhere before? I've been
to some appalling places.

❧ That girl's been on more laps than a napkin.

❧ Why, do you get more intelligent outside?
Or
I prefer to insult you in comfort, thanks.
Or
I'll say it again very slowly for you.

(*On being asked to step outside to repeat a remark.*)

❧ You have an hourglass figure; pity the sand settled in the wrong place.

❧ Can you count to twenty without taking off your shoes?

⚞ Seriousness is stupidity sent to college.

P. J. O'ROURKE (1947–)
American writer

⚞ Old blondes never fade – they just dye away.

⚞ Not all men are annoying – some are
dead . . .

⚞ She's aged more than her husband – but
less often.

⚞ You dress for the nuclear age – there's too
much fall-out.

⚞ You know how to hang on to your youth –
you never introduce him to other women.

⚞ If I threw you a stick, would you leave?

⚞ An empty taxi stopped – and you got out.
(originally said of Jack Warner,
the film mogul)

⚞ Sorry , dear, but a man has to do something
to relieve the monogamy.

⚞ If God had meant us to walk around naked, he would never have invented the wicker chair.

ERMA BOMBECK
American writer

⚞ God is not dead – just working on a less ambitious project.

⚞ Give a man a free hand, and he'll run it all over you.

ATTRIBUTED TO MAE WEST (1892–1980)
American actress

Money, aspiration and social pratfalls

What a pity times are no longer what they used to be! Children no longer obey their parents and everyone wants to write a book.

Inscribed on the oldest piece of papyrus in Istanbul's State Museum

Nycilla dyes her locks, 'tis said,
But 'tis a foul aspersion;
She buys them black; they therefore need
No subsequent immersion.

MARCUS VALERIUS MARTIAL (*c.* AD 40–102)
Roman poet

This was a good dinner enough, to be sure; but it was not a dinner to ask a man to.

DR SAMUEL JOHNSON (1709–1784)
English author and lexicographer

I like him and his wife. He is so ladylike, and she is such a perfect gentleman.

SYDNEY SMITH (1771–1845)
English clergyman and essayist

There goes Jim Fisk, with his hands in his own pockets for a change.

ANONYMOUS
on financier James Fisk

The golf links lie so near the mill
That almost every day
The labouring children can look out
And see the men at play.

SARAH CLEGHORN (1876–1959)
American poet

'I am thinking of buying a yacht myself –
  Tell me, what is the upkeep?'
J. P. MORGAN: 'Anybody who has to ask that
can't afford one.'

❧ . . . But to return to Lord Granby. He
carried his length of limb rather lankily,
but he had a beautiful Christ-like face
that seemed curiously out of place
in the British aristocracy.

GERTRUDE ATHERTON
in Adventures of a Novelist

❧ He is the tenth possessor of a foolish face.

DAVID LLOYD GEORGE (1863–1945)
British prime minister,
on any member of the aristocracy

❧ To mankind in general, Macbeth and Lady Macbeth stand out as the supreme type of all that a host and hostess should not be.

MAX BEERBOHM (1872–1956)
British writer and caricaturist

❧ If you pick up a starving dog and make him prosperous, he will not bite you. This is the principal difference between a dog and a man.

MARK TWAIN (1835–1910)
American writer

❧ Geta from wool and weaving first began
Swelling and swelling to a Gentleman;
When he was a Gentleman and bravely
    dight,
He left not swelling till he was a knight:
At last (forgetting what he was at first)
He swole to be a lord, and then he burst.

THOMAS BASTARD (1566–1618)
on an aspirant weaver

❧ Prince Albert shot ninety-six rabbits in the
Royal preserves. The animals, anxious for
the honour of seeing the Prince, fell the
unhappy victims of a too fatal curiosity.

COMIC ALMANACK

❧ On one occasion Dr Butler (former Master of Trinity) wrote to Sir Robert Scott, addressing his envelope to The Master, St John's College, next door to Trinity College, Cambridge.

Sir Robert was unperturbed. He wrote his reply to The Master, Trinity College, opposite Matthew's the grocer's, Cambridge.

G. W.,
Spectator

❧ The English country-gentleman galloping after a fox – the unspeakable in full pursuit of the uneatable.

OSCAR WILDE (1856–1900)
British dramatist and poet

A friend I met some half-hour since –
'Good morrow, Jack!' quoth I;
The new-made Knight, like any Prince,
Frown'd, nodded and passed by;
When up came Jem – 'Sir John, your
Slave!'
'Ah James; we dine at eight –
Fail not – (low bows the supple knave)
Don't make my lady wait.'
The King can do no wrong? As I'm a
sinner,
He's spoilt an honest tradesman and my
dinner.

INGOLDSBY LEGENDS
imitating Martial (c. AD 40–102), Roman poet

୧୦ HENRY IRVING (*getting into a hansom cab*):
Drive me home.
CAB DRIVER: Yes, sir, what address?
IRVING: Why should I tell the address
of my beautiful home to a common
fellow like you?

୧୦ I don't want to belong to any club that
would accept me as one of its members.

GROUCHO MARX
resigning from the Friars Club

୧୦ Social tact is making your company feel at
home even though you wish they were.

ANONYMOUS

❧ All the spoons of the nation soon made
　　known their wishes,
　To be speedily plunged in Her Majesty's
　　dishes:
　Yet 'twas found to be useless to take any
　　more,
　For the spoonies at Court were too many
　　before.

On the presentation of a wooden spoon
to Queen Victoria

❧ I told him to take a picture of his testicles so
that he'd have something to remember them
by if he ever hit me again.

BOBBY KNIGHT
American basketball coach

❧ 'Hot, smoking hot,' On the fire was a pot
   Well replenish'd, but really I can't say with
      what;
   For, famed as the French always are for
      ragouts,
   No creature can tell what they put in their
      stews,
   Whether bull-frogs, old gloves, or old wigs,
      or old shoes.

THOMAS INGOLDSBY (1788–1845)
English humorist, 'The Bagman's Dog'

❧ Heaven shall forgive you Bridge at dawn,
   The clothes you wear – or do not wear –
   And Ladies' Leap-frog on the lawn
   And dyes and drugs and petits verres.
   Your vicious things melt in air . . .
   But for the Virtuous Things you do,
   The Righteous Work, the Public Care,
   It shall not be forgiven you.

G. K. CHESTERTON (1874–1936)
English writer, 'Ballade d'une Grande Dame'

❧ Fish and visitors spoil after the third day.

TRADITIONAL SAYING

∽ Mrs Patrick Campbell visited a certain movie mogul's house in Hollywood. He asked her to sign the visitor's book when leaving. She wrote: ' "Quoth the Raven" Stella Campbell'.

∽ A local doctor's bill now bears a sticker reading, 'Long time no fee'.

∽ We thought he was a bit of an aristocrat when he first came, but we soon found he was a decent fellow.

Factory workers describing their managing director, in Picture Post

❧ My colleagues of the Film Division of the
Ministry of Information were as nice a
bunch of boys and girls as ever wore
corduroy. I suppose most of them earned
their livings before the war, but I cannot
for the life of me imagine how.

GERALD KERSH
in 'Clean, Bright and Slightly Oiled'

❧ When the police called they looked so
frightening she thought they were
gangsters or insurance people.

OLD BAILEY WITNESS

❧ Kitchens are dominated by rissole merchants. The single, boiled potato nestles close to the stringy beans in the vegetable dish. Sausage toad, savoury steak, and that most supreme of insults . . . 'supreme de cod', still lord it on the menu.

EVENING STANDARD

❧ My son Kenneth was entertaining a friend who is a year younger (five and a half). The younger boy said: 'We've got a telephone and a fridge and a television. You haven't got much, have you?' To which my boy replied: 'I've got manners.'

MRS COLLINS
letter to the Daily Mirror

 ❧ Only a starving nation would willingly tolerate having to get a licence to replace a lavatory pan cracked by frost, or tolerate that a man with an amputated leg must get a medical certificate to state that the leg had not regrown each time he wants certain extra allowances.

DR FRANKLIN BICKNELL

 ❧ There are the judges robed and wigged and looking from the gallery, if one can say so without disrespect, like a flock of sheep – pedigree sheep, of course.

Manchester Guardian
*on the opening of a new session
at the House of Lords*

Party put-downs and flirtation follies

∾ Heat, ma'am? It was so dreadful here that I found there was nothing left for it but to take off my flesh and sit in my bones.

SYDNEY SMITH (1771–1845)
English clergyman and essayist

∾ Why do you sit there looking like an envelope without any address on it?

MARK TWAIN (1835–1910)
American writer

∾ I'm busy now. Can I ignore you some other time?

ANONYMOUS

❧ *This agreeable Actress in the Part of Sir Harry coming into the Greenroom said pleasantly,* In my Conscience, I believe half the Men in the House take me for one of their own Sex. *Another Actress reply'd* It may be so, but in my Conscience the other half can convince them to the Contrary.

WILLIAM RUFUS CHETWOOD
eighteenth-century author and publisher,
on actress Peg Woffington

❧ Keep talking. I always yawn when I'm interested.

ANONYMOUS

❧ Call me. You can find my number and name in the telephone book.

❧ LORD NORTHCLIFFE (*to a scrawny Bernard Shaw*): The trouble with you, Shaw, is that you look as if there were a famine in the land.
SHAW (*to the obese Northcliffe*):
The trouble with you, Northcliffe, is that you look as if you were the cause of it.

❧ Excuse me, I think you have mistaken me
for someone who gives a shit . . .

A beautiful woman to a rather moist-looking
man, overheard at a party in New York

❧ If you know how to please a woman,
then please leave me alone.

ANONYMOUS

❧ If the phone doesn't ring,
you'll know it's me.

ANONYMOUS

❧ No one can have a higher opinion of
  him than I have – and I think he is
  a dirty little beast.

W. S. GILBERT (1836–1911)
English librettist

❧ I must decline your invitation owing to
  a subsequent engagement.

OSCAR WILDE (1856–1900)
British dramatist and poet

❧ Please could you ask me out from a little
  further away? Your breath is bleaching
  my eyebrows.

ANONYMOUS

❧ Sure, if you saw me naked, you'd die happy
– but if I saw you naked, I'd die laughing.

ANONYMOUS

❧ A revolting woman simpered up to me and
said, 'I hear you are writing a book. Won't
you please bring me into it.' To get rid of
her I promised I would. This paragraph
shows that I keep my promises.

VERNON BARTLETT (1894–1983)
English writer, from Go East, Old Man

❧ My body is my temple, but there are no
services for the desperate . . .

ANONYMOUS

❧ The other day a man came to dinner and I
said to him, 'You've been here before?' –

'Yes,' said the man.

'And,' I conjectured, thinking hard, 'it
must have been some two years ago?'

'No,' said the man, 'You aren't quite
right, it was at tea-time.'

JOHN FOTHERGILL
twentieth-century eccentric
English restaurateur and writer

❧ The girls are so beautiful, it's sad to think
that twenty years from now, they'll all be
five years older!

WILL ROGERS (1879–1935)

❧ What do you do for a living? As for myself,
I'm a female impersonator.

ANONYMOUS
put-down to banal pick-up line

❧ I have never liked bargains when it came
to sex.

HEDY LAMARR

❧ Would I like to go back to your place? I'm
not sure. Will two people fit under a rock?

ANONYMOUS

❧ She looks like an accident on its way
to happen.

ANONYMOUS PARTY GUEST

❧ Fine words – I wonder where you
stole them.

JONATHAN SWIFT (1667–1745)
English satirist

❧ Interesting pick-up line. Do you write
your own material or just scribble it?

ANONYMOUS

❧ I'm thrilled to hear that you would go to
the end of the world for me. Would you
go now – and stay there?

ANONYMOUS

❧ No, the 't' is silent – as in Harlow.

MARGOT ASQUITH (1864–1945)
*prime ministerial wife, to film star Jean Harlow,
on being asked the pronunciation of her name*

❧ The affair between Margot Asquith and
Margot Asquith will live as one of the
prettiest love stories in all literature.

DOROTHY PARKER (1893–1967)
American writer

Any part of you that touches me, you're
not getting back.

Save your breath – you'll need it to inflate
your date.

If you were the last man left alive, I'm
sorry but humanity would be a goner.

❧ Unshagalicious

ANONYMOUS

❧ I married beneath me – all women do.

NANCY ASTOR (1879 –1964)
the first woman
Member of Parliament in Britain

❧ Excuse me, my leg has gone to sleep – do you mind if I join it?

ALEXANDER WOOLCOTT (1887–1943)
to a bore at a party

❧ In order to avoid being called a flirt, she
   always yielded easily.

CHARLES MAURICE DE TALLEYRAND (1754–1838)
French politician

❧ I'd love to go out with you next Saturday,
   but I have a previous appointment which I
   will arrange as soon as possible.

ANONYMOUS

❧ Sorry, I don't date outside my species.

ANONYMOUS

❧ (*On being asked for a date*) I see you've decided to humiliate yourself in public . . .

· ANONYMOUS

Lousy liaisons and awful anatomies

❧ You say all the girls are on fire for you?
You, with a face like a man swimming
under water?

MARCUS VALERIUS MARTIAL (_c._ AD 40–102)
Roman poet

❧ Have you not reason then to bee ashamed,
and to forbeare this filthie noveltie . . .
custome loathsome to the eye, hatefull to
the nose, harmfull to the braine, dangerous
to the Lungs, and in the blacke stinking
fume thereof, nearest resembling the
horrible Stigian smoke of the pit that is
bottomlesse.

JAMES I (1566–1625)
Counterblast to Tobacco

❧ Arrant, malmsey-nose knave!

WILLIAM SHAKESPEARE (1564–1616)
English dramatist, Henry IV Part 2

❧ Your virginity, your old virginity, is like
one of our French wither'd pears: it
looks ill, it eats drily.

WILLIAM SHAKESPEARE (1564–1616)
All's Well That Ends Well

❧ Man and wife make one fool.

BEN JONSON (1572–1637)
English dramatist

❧ With leering Looks, Bull-fac'd, and
                                     freckl'd fair,
With two left legs, and Judas-color'd Hair,
And frowzy Pores that taint the ambient Air.

JOHN DRYDEN (1631–1700)
English poet, on publisher Jacob Tonson

❧ One fool at least in every married couple.

HENRY FIELDING (1707–1754)
English novelist

❧ Your mouth is puckered and looks like
a heap of house dust.

TRADITIONAL YORUBA INSULT

❧ If he were a horse, nobody would buy him.

WALTER BAGEHOT (1826–1877)
English economist and journalist,
on Lord Brougham

❧ The Bible says that the last thing God made was woman. He must have made her on a Saturday night – it shows fatigue.

ALEXANDRE DUMAS (FILS) (1824–1895)
French writer

❧ He might have bought an action against his countenance for libel and recovered heavy damages.

CHARLES DICKENS (1812–1870)
English novelist

❧ She had a face on her that'd fade flowers.

GEORGE ADE (1866–1944)

❧ NOËL COWARD, *to* EDNA FERBER: Edna, you look almost like a man.
FERBER: So do you.

He was so ugly he hurt my feelings.

JACKIE 'MOMS' MABLEY

Modesty has ruined more kidneys than bad liquor.

DR S. MORRIS

What time he can spare from the adornment of his person he devotes to the neglect of his duties.

BENJAMIN JOWETT (1817–1893)
English scholar, describing an undergraduate pupil

&. Going to marry her! Impossible! You mean, a part of her; he could not marry her all himself. It would be a case not of bigamy, but of trigamy . . . You might people a colony with her; or give an assembly with her; or perhaps take your morning walks around her . . . Or you might read the Riot Act and disperse her; in short, you might do anything with her but marry her.

SYDNEY SMITH (1771–1845)
English clergyman and essayist, on the proposed marriage of a young acquaintance to an overweight widow

What a hideous, odd-looking man Sydney Smith is! With a mouth like an oyster, and three double-chins.

MRS BROOKFIELD

She may well pass for forty-three in the dusk with the light behind her.

W. S. GILBERT (1836–1911)
English librettist

A woman whose face looked as if it had been made out of sugar and someone had licked it.

GEORGE BERNARD SHAW (1856–1950)
Anglo-Irish dramatist, on Isadora Duncan

❧ Sex with a man is all right, but it's not as good as the real thing.

ANONYMOUS GRAFFITO

❧ He had but one eye, and the popular prejudice runs in favour of two.

CHARLES DICKENS (1812–1870)

❧ She sounds more and more like Donald Duck.

BETTE DAVIS
on Katherine Hepburn

෪ I have eyes like a bullfrog, a neck like an
   ostrich and long limp hair. You must have
   to be good to survive with that equipment.

BETTE DAVIS

෪ She knows how to please a man.
   She sleeps on the couch.

ANONYMOUS

෪ He must have had a magnificent build
   before his stomach went in for a career
   of its own.

MARGARET HALSEY

ʘ Two women seldom grow intimate but at the expense of a third person.

JONATHAN SWIFT (1667–1745)
English satirist

ʘ One can find women who have never had one love affair, but it is rare indeed to find a woman who has only had one.

FRANÇOIS LA ROCHEFOUCAULD (1613–1680)
French writer

ʘ Frankly I've had more fun sitting a spin-dryer . . .

ANONYMOUS
from a disgruntled woman to her man

❧ Cocaine is God's way of telling you that you are making too much money.

ROBIN WILLIAMS
Hollywood film actor

❧ A very little wit is valued in a woman, as we are pleased with a few words spoken plain by a parrot.

JONATHAN SWIFT (1667–1745)

❧ It's like trying to hammer a six-inch nail into a concrete wall with a dead fish.

ANONYMOUS GRAFFITO
about the vexations of sexual intercourse

ʘ It seems to me that when a woman is
wearing shorts her charms are enlarged
without being enhanced.

BEVERLEY NICHOLS

ʘ Frankly my vibrator is bigger than that –
and it has a higher IQ.

ANONYMOUS

ʘ He named his penis Wilberforce so as to
be on first name terms with the person
who took all the decisions.

ANONYMOUS

❧ Frankly, said the disappointed woman to
   her lover, I've seen more meat on a
   vegetarian's toothpick than on your dong.

   Legendary insult in the sex wars.

❧ Oh goody. We're going to have sex. I'll get
   out the tweezers and the magnifying glass.

   *Another remark designed for
   instant detumescence*

❧ Teenagers are God's punishment for
   having sex.

PATRICK MURRAY

∞ Instead of getting married again, I'm going to find a woman I don't like, and give her a house.

LEWIS GRIZZARD (1946–1996)
American Southern humorist

∞ If you have the presence of mind, here is what you are supposed to do if you are a woman to whom a man is exposing himself. You peer at the offending object with scholarly disdain and say: 'Golly, that's cute. It's just like a penis – only much smaller.'

ॐ He looked at me as if I was a side-dish he hadn't ordered.

RING LARDNER (1885–1933)
American short story writer

ॐ Her face was her chaperone.

RUPERT HUGHES

ॐ An Irish homosexual is one who prefers women to drink.

SEAN O'FAOLAIN (1900–1991)
Irish writer

An Irishman is the only man in the world who will step over the bodies of a dozen naked women to get to a bottle of stout.

ANONYMOUS

Why dost thou converse with that trunk of humours, that bolting-hutch of beastliness, that swoln parcel of dropsies, that huge bombard of sack, that stuffed cloakbag of guts, that roasted Manningtree ox with the pudding in his belly, that reverend vice, that greay iniquity, that father ruffian, that vanity in years?

WILLIAM SHAKESPEARE (1564–1616)
Henry IV, Part 2

⁎ If only he'd wash his neck, I'd wring it.

ANONYMOUS

⁎ Women's intuition is the result of millions of years of not thinking.

RUPERT HUGHES

⁎ The King blew his nose twice, and wiped the royal perspiration repeatedly from a face which is probably the largest uncivilized spot in England.

OLIVER WENDELL HOLMES (1809–1894)
American writer, on William IV

∝ Would thou wert clean enough to
spit upon.

WILLIAM SHAKESPEARE (1564–1616)

∝ Deformed Sir, The Ugly Club in full meeting
have elected you an honorary Member . . .
Falstaff was fat, Thersites was hunchbacked,
and Slowkenlergus was renowned for the
eminent miscalculation which Nature had
made in the length of the nose; but it
remained for you to unite all species of
deformity and stand forth the Prince
of Ugly Fellows.

Letter to Abraham Lincoln

❧ . . . the face, with the long proboscis, the
   protruding teeth of the Apocalyptic horse . . .

GEORGE MEREDITH (1828–1909)
English novelist and poet, on George Eliot

❧ Most women are not as young as they
   are painted.

MAX BEERBOHM (1872–1956)
English writer and caricaturist

❧ Love is the delightful interval between
   meeting a beautiful girl and discovering
   that she looks like a haddock.

JOHN BARRYMORE (1882–1942)
American actor

❧ Why don't you get a haircut? You look
like a chrysanthemum.

P. G. WODEHOUSE (1881–1975)
English novelist

❧ She got her good looks from her father.
He's a plastic surgeon.

GROUCHO MARX

❧ A plumber's idea of Cleopatra.

W. C. FIELDS (1880–1946)
American comic actor, on Mae West

❧ A blank helpless sort of face, rather like a
rose just before you drench it in DDT.

JOHN CAREY
Sunday Times, *on Diana Cooper*

❧ The feminine vanity case is the grave of
masculine illusions.

HELEN ROWLAND

❧ A dilapidated macaw . . .

EDITH SITWELL (1887–1964)
English poet, on Lady Mary Wortley Montagu

❧ Mr Lawrence looked like a plaster gnome
on a stone toadstool in some suburban
garden . . . He looked as if he had just
returned from spending an uncomfortable
night in a very dark cave.

EDITH SITWELL
on D. H. Lawrence

❧ Pale, marmoreal Eliot was there last week,
like a chapped office boy on a high stool,
with a cold in his head.

VIRGINIA WOOLF (1882–1941)
English novelist, on T. S. Eliot

℮ I do not think I have ever seen a nastier-
looking man . . . Under the black hat,
when I had first seen them, the eyes had
been those of an unsuccessful rapist.

ERNEST HEMINGWAY (1899–1961)
American writer, on Wyndham Lewis

℮ A typical triumph of modern science to find
the only part of Randolph that was not
malignant – and remove it.

EVELYN WAUGH (1903–1966)
English novelist, describing an operation on
Randolph Churchill to remove a lump that
proved benign

❧ I never forget a face, but in your case I'll make an exception.

GROUCHO MARX

❧ Fotherington-thomas . . . skipping like a girlie he is utterly wet and a sissy. He reads chatterbox chiz and we suspeckt that he kepes dollies at home. Anyway his favourite character is little lord fauntleroy and when I sa he hav a face like a tomato he repli I forgiv you molesworth for those uncouth words.

GEOFFREY WILLANS AND RONALD SEARLE
Down With Skool!

❧ Unspeakable, like a hedgehog all in primroses.

NANCY MITFORD (1904–1973)
English novelist, describing Princess Margaret

❧ I have seen better-looking faces on pirate flags.

ANONYMOUS
on Alec Douglas-Home

❧ The Russians love Brooke Shields because her eyebrows remind them of Leonid Brezhnev.

ROBIN WILLIAMS

❧ She has the face of an exhausted gnu.

JOHN SYMON
on Anjelica Huston

❧ Barbara Cartland's eyes were twin miracles
of mascara and looked like two small crows
that had crashed into a chalk cliff.

CLIVE JAMES
Australian journalist and writer

❧ A monstrous carbuncle on the face of a
much-loved and elegant friend.

PRINCE CHARLES (1949–)
*heir to the British throne, denouncing a proposed
extension to London's National Gallery*

≈ He's so low he can't kiss a tumblebug's
gilliwinkle without bending his knees.

ANONYMOUS

≈ They claim to be he-men, but the hair from
their combined chests wouldn't have made
a wig for a grape.

ROBERT BENCHLEY (1889–1945)

≈ My face looks like a wedding cake left out
in the rain.

W.H.AUDEN (1907–1973)
English poet

∽ He looks as if he'd been weaned on a pickle.

ALICE ROOSEVELT LONGWORTH (1893–1967)
*daughter of President Teddy Roosevelt, on
Calvin Coolidge*

∽ If you can't say anything good about
anybody, sit right down here beside me.

ALICE ROOSEVELT LONGWORTH (1893–1967)

∽ The more I see of men, the more I like dogs.

MADAME DE STAËL (1766–1817)
French writer

Sport – war without much bloodshed

❧ A man described as a sportsman is generally
a bookmaker who takes actresses to night
clubs.

JIMMY CANNON (1910–1973)
American sports writer

❧ Aye, they say the new striker I'm opposing
is fast – but how fast can he limp?

MICK McCARTHY
Irish football player

❧ Joggers are basically neurotic, bony, smug
types who could bore the paint off a DC–10.

RICK REILLY

❧ I do not participate in any sport that has ambulances at the bottom of the hill.

ERMA BOMBECK

❧ Jon Snow is approaching the wicket like Groucho Marx stalking a waitress . . .

JOHN ARLOTT
cricket commentator,
describing the test-match bowler

❧ Like a Volvo, Bjorn Borg is rugged, has good after-sales service and is very dull.

CLIVE JAMES (1939–)
Australian journalist and writer

♪ They should call it a swimming 'ool'
because the 'p' is silent.

PATRICK MURRAY

♪ Managing a baseball team is like trying to
make chicken salad out of chicken shit.

JOE KULEL

♪ A sportsman is a man who every now
and then simply has to go out and
kill something.

STEPHEN LEACOCK (1869–1944)
Canadian political economist

❧ Ballet is the fairies' baseball.

OSCAR LEVANT (1906–1972)
American pianist and author

❧ The fascination of shooting depends almost
entirely on whether you are the right or
wrong end of the gun.

P. G. WODEHOUSE (1881–1975)
English novelist

❧ He is so brave, but such a moaner. He
should have 'Who Dares Whines'
embroidered on his overalls.

SIMON BARNES
English columnist, on Nigel Mansell, racing driver

❧ The drunk we could all have become.

MICHAEL HERD
*English journalist, on George Best,
legendary Irish footballer and drunk*

❧ Waddling around like a recently impregnated hippopotamus . . . Paul Gascoigne has become a bona fide wobble-bottom. But should football finally fail him, at least there's a whole range of alternative careers now on the horizon. Father Christmas . . . barrage balloon . . . spacehopper.

MARCUS BERKMANN
Independent on Sunday

❧ The minute a man is convinced he's interesting, he isn't.

STEPHEN LEACOCK
Canadian economist

❧ Whatever you may be sure of, be sure of this: that you are dreadfully like other people.

JAMES RUSSELL LOWELL (1819–1891)
American editor and poet

Vanity, vanity —
all is vanity

∾ The last time I saw him, he was walking down Lover's Lane holding his own hand.

FRED ALLEN (1894–1956)
American radio comedian

∾ There but for the grace of God, goes God.

SIR WINSTON CHURCHILL (1874–1965)
British prime minister

∾ One nice thing about egotists: they don't talk about other people.

GEORGE CARLIN
American comedian

❧ There was an actress who gave a dazzling half-hour monologue about herself at a post-performance theatrical party. Suddenly waking up to what she was doing, she said: 'But enough about me. Tell me, what did *you* think of my performance?'

❧ He is a self-made man and worships his creator.

JOHN BRIGHT (1811–1889)
British politician

❧ Well, at least he has found his true love – what a pity he can't marry himself.

FRANK SINATRA
on Robert Redford

❧ If there's anything more important than my ego around, I want it caught and shot now.

DOUGLAS ADAMS (1952–2001)
British writer

❧ Nobody can be exactly like me. Even I have trouble doing it.

TALLULAH BANKHEAD (1903–1968)
American actress

❧ An egotist is a person of low taste – more interested in himself than in me.

AMBROSE BIERCE (1842–1914)
American writer and journalist

⁋ Big egos are big shields for lots of
empty space.

DIANA BLACK
twentieth-century American writer

⁋ I may not be totally perfect, but parts of me
are excellent.

ASHLEIGH BRILLIANT (1933–)
American humorous aphorist

⁋ The smaller the mind the greater
the conceit.

AESOP (SIXTH CENTURY BC)
Greek fabulist

❧ When they discover the centre of the universe, a lot of people will be disappointed to discover they are not it.

BERNARD BAILEY
American humorist

❧ Conceit is God's gift to little men.

BRUCE BARTON (1886–1967)
American author and advertising man

❧ An ostentatious man will rather relate a blunder or an absurdity he has committed, than be debarred from talking of his own dear person.

JOSEPH ADDISON (1672–1719)
English essayist

❧ We are so vain that we even care for the opinion of those we don't care for.

MARIE EBNER VON ESCHENBACH (1830–1916)
Austrian novelist

❧ I feel like I'm the best, but you're not going to get me to say that.

JERRY RICE

❧ The greatest of faults, I should say, is to be conscious of none.

THOMAS CARLYLE (1795–1881)
Scottish historian

❧ Everyone wants to be Cary Grant. Even I want to be Cary Grant.

CARY GRANT
Hollywood film star

❧ I have nothing to declare but my genius.

OSCAR WILDE (1856–1900)
British dramatist and poet

∾ Pride: the vice of the lowest and most debased creatures no less than of the high and self-assured. The miserable companion of thieves and ruffians, the fallen outcast of low haunts, the associate of the scourings of the jails and hulks, living within the shadow of the gallows itself.

CHARLES DICKENS (1812–1870)
English novelist

∾ When did I realize I was God? Well, I was praying and I suddenly realized I was talking to myself.

PETER O'TOOLE
English actor

∞ She laughs at everything you say. Why?
Because she has fine teeth.

BENJAMIN FRANKLIN (1706–1790)
American statesman and scientist

∞ Egotism is the anaesthetic that dulls the
pain of stupidity.

FRANK LEAHY (1907–1973)
American football coach

∞ I have been complimented many times and
they always embarrass me; I always feel that
they have not said enough.

MARK TWAIN (1835–1910)
American writer

 ❧ She thinks she's a siren, but she looks more like a false alarm.

ANONYMOUS

 ❧ He knows when an idea is good – when it's one of his own.

ANONYMOUS

 ❧ He always wants to be the centre of attention. When he goes to a funeral, he's sorry he isn't the corpse.

ANONYMOUS

Matters legal & medical

❧ The first thing we do, let's kill all
the lawyers.

WILLIAM SHAKESPEARE (1564–1616)
English dramatist, Henry IV Part 2

❧ God works wonders now and then; behold,
a lawyer, an honest man.

BENJAMIN FRANKLIN (1706–1790)
American statesman and scientist

❧ He is no lawyer who cannot take two sides.

CHARLES LAMB (1775–1834)
English essayist

❧ Lawyers earn a living by the sweat of their browbeating.

JAMES HUNEKER (1860–1921)
American music critic

❧ A man may as well open an oyster without a knife as a lawyer's mouth without a fee.

BARTEN HOLYDAY
Technogamia, *1618*

❧ A lawyer is a learned gentleman who rescues your estate from your enemies and keeps it himself.

LORD HENRY BROUGHAM (1778–1868)
English politician

❧ LAWYER (to a Long Island courtroom):
Gentlemen, I sincerely hope your decision
will not be influenced by the Chesterfieldian
urbanity of my opponent.
CHOATE: Gentlemen, I am sure you will not
be influenced, either, by the
Westchesterfieldian suburbanity of my
opponent.

JOSEPH H. CHOATE (1832–1917)
American politician

❧ Lawyers are the only persons in whom
ignorance of the law is not punished.

JEREMY BENTHAM (1748–1832)
English philosopher

JUDGE: I am sorry, Mr Smith, but I am none the wiser.

SMITH: No, my Lord. But you are better informed.

F. E. SMITH (1872–1930)
English lawyer, having concisely summarized a piece of evidence in vain

Two young women who had not seen each since their school days met up again in a bar. 'Well,' said one, ' I married a lawyer and an honest man.'

'Gosh,' said her friend, 'isn't that bigamy?'

❧ Why do laboratories use lawyers and not
   rats in scientific experiments?
   (1) There are more lawyers
   (2) The technical staff do not form
        attachments to them
   (3) You can get the lawyers to do things
        that the rats will not do . . .

❧ Beneath this smooth stone by the
                        bone of his bone
   Sleeps Master John Gill;
   By lies when alive this attorney did thrive,
   And now that he's dead he lies still.

ANONYMOUS EPITAPH

❧ For certain people, after fifty, litigation tales the place of sex.

GORE VIDAL (1927–)
American novelist

❧ The extreme penalty for bigamy? Two mothers-in-law.

LORD CHIEF JUSTICE RUSSELL

❧ Q: What do you call a Scouser [a native of Liverpool] wearing a suit?
   A: The defendant.

ANONYMOUS

❧ Lawyer (*noun*): One skilled in the circumvention of the law.
Lawsuit (*noun*): A machine which you go into as a pig and come out of as a sausage.

AMBROSE BIERCE (1842–1914)
American writer and journalist

❧ I think we may class the lawyer in the natural history of monsters.

JOHN KEATS (1795–1821)
English poet

❧ A man who is his own lawyer has a fool for a client.

ANONYMOUS

❧ When you have no basis for argument in
law, abuse the plaintiff.

MARCUS TULLIUS CICERO (106–43 BC)
Roman orator, statesman and man of letters

❧ English Law: where there are two
alternatives: one intelligent, one stupid;
one attractive, one vulgar; one noble, one
ape-like; one serious and sincere, one
undignified and false; one far-sighted,
one short; everybody will invariably
choose the latter.

CYRIL CONNOLLY (1903–1975)
English literary critic

∞ Doctors are the same as lawyers; the only difference is that lawyers merely rob you, whereas doctors rob and kill you too.

ANTON CHEKHOV (1860–1904)
Russian writer and playwright

∞ The Honest Lawyer
Name of a pub in the county of Norfolk

∞ Judges, as a class, display, in a matter of arranging alimony, that reckless generosity which is found only in men giving away someone else's money.

P. G. WODEHOUSE (1881–1975)
English novelist

❧ To call him grey would be an insult to porridge.

SIR NICHOLAS FAIRBAIRN
*politician, on Lord Hope, an austere
Scottish judge*

❧ The art of medicine consists of amusing the patient while nature cures the disease.

FRANÇOIS MARIE AROUET DE VOLTAIRE
(1694–1778)
French philosopher and writer

⚞ I've decided to skip 'holistic'. I don't know
   what it means, and don't want to know.
   This may seem extreme, bit I've followed the
   same strategy with 'Gestalt' and the 'Twist',
   and lived to tell the tale.

CALVIN TRILLIN (1935–)
American columnist

⚞ He's a devout believer in the department of
   witchcraft called medical science.

GEORGE BERNARD SHAW (1856–1950)
Anglo-Irish dramatist

❧ Doctors pour drugs of which they
know little to cure diseases of which
they know less into human beings of
whom they know nothing.

FRANÇOIS MARIE AROUET DE VOLTAIRE
(1694–1778)

❧ Doctors will have more lives to answer for in
the next world than even we generals.

NAPOLEON BONAPARTE (1769–1821)
Emperor of the French

❧ He has been a doctor for a year now and has had two patients – no, three, I think – yes, it was three. I attended their funerals.

MARK TWAIN (1835–1910)
American writer

❧ A doctor gets no pleasure out of the health of his friends.

MICHEL EYQUEM DE MONTAIGNE (1553–1592)
French essayist

❧ There are more old drunkards than there are old doctors.

BENJAMIN FRANKLIN (1706–1790)

❧ He was once a doctor, but now he is an
   undertaker; and what he does as an
   undertaker he used to do as a doctor.

MARCUS VALERIUS MARTIAL (*c.* AD 40–102)
Roman poet

❧ Dr— well remembered that he had a salary
   to receive and only forgot that he had
   a duty to perform.

EDWARD GIBBON (1737–1794)
English historian

Many a diabetic has stayed alive by stealing the bread denied to him by his doctor . . . Half the modern drugs could well be thrown out of the window, except that the birds might eat them.

MARTIN HENRY FISCHER (b. 1879)
American author and scientist

The best doctor is the one you run for and cannot find.

DENIS DIDEROT (1713–1784)
French philosopher and encyclopaedist

Religion and
other vices

༄ Religion is the venereal disease of mankind.

HENRI DE MONTHERLANT (1896–1972)
French novelist and playwright

༄ The trouble with born-again Christians is
that they are an even bigger pain the
second time around.

HERB CAEN (1916–)
San Francisco columnist

༄ Religion: a comfort for the hard-of-thinking.

ANONYMOUS

❧ Her soul was like some quaggy latrine into which every imaginable iniquity had flowed.

LUCIUS APULEIUS (*born c.* AD 123)
Roman poet, Metamorphoses

❧ Anger makes dull men witty, but it keeps them poor.

FRANCES BACON (1561–1626)
English philosopher and politician

❧ Perhaps the most revolting character the United States ever produced was the Christian Businessman.

H. L. MENCKEN (1880–1956)
American editor and writer

๛ The Bible tells us to love our neighbours,
and also to love our enemies; probably
because they are generally the same people.

G. K. CHESTERTON (1874–1936)
English writer

๛ He will crush out your blood, and make it
fly, and it shall be sprinkled on His
garments, so as to stain all His raiment. He
will not only hate you, but He will have you
in the utmost contempt; no place shall be
fit for you but under His feet to be trodden
down as the mire of the streets.

JONATHAN EDWARDS
American preacher, to his congregation

୧ My prayer to God is a very short one: 'O Lord, make my enemies ridiculous.' God has granted it.

FRANÇOIS MARIE AROUET DE VOLTAIRE
(1694–1778)
French philosopher and writer

୧ In the Church, if you are not well born, you must be very base or very foolish, or both.

SYDNEY SMITH (1771–1845)
English clergyman and essayist

∾ If Jesus Christ were to come today, people would not even crucify him. They would invite Him to dinner, and hear what He had to say, and make fun of it.

THOMAS CARLYLE (1795–1881)
Scottish historian

∾ Poor Matt. He's gone to heaven, no doubt – but he won't like God.

ROBERT LOUIS STEVENSON (1850–1894)
Scottish writer, on Matthew Arnold

❧ Truly religious people are resigned to everything, even to mediocre poetry.

OSCAR WILDE (1856–1900)
British dramatist and poet

❧ All religions issue Bibles against Satan, and say most injurious things about him, but we never hear his side.

MARK TWAIN (1835–1900)
American writer

❧ Show me a woman who doesn't feel guilt and I'll show you a man.

ERICA JONG

❧ We have just enough religion to make us
hate but not enough to make us love
one another.

JONATHAN SWIFT (1667–1745)
English satirist

❧ One should forgive one's enemies, but not
before they are hanged.

HEINRICH HEINE (1797–1856)
German poet

❧ All religions are founded on the fear of the
many and the cleverness of the few.

STENDHAL (1783–1842)
French novelist

No, it is better not. She would only ask me to take a message to Albert.

BENJAMIN DISRAELI (1804–1881)
British prime minister, when dying – on hearing that Queen Victoria proposed to visit him.

No people do so much harm as those who go about doing good.

MANDELL CREIGHTON (1843–1901)
British bishop and historian

Which is it? Is man one of God's blunders, or is God one of man's blunders?

FRIEDRICH NIETZSCHE (1844–1900)
German philosopher

⅋ There is sufficiency in the world for man's need but not for man's greed.

MAHATMA GANDHI (1869–1948)
Indian leader

⅋ The Church has always been ready to swap off treasures in heaven for cash down.

ROBERT GREEN INGERSOLL (1833–1899)
American lawyer

⅋ The easy confidence with which I know another man's religion is folly teaches me to suspect that my own is also.

MARK TWAIN (1835–1910)

છે Good people sleep better than bad people,
but bad people enjoy the waking hours
much more.

WOODY ALLEN

છે You never see animals going through the
absurd and often horrible fooleries of magic
and religion. Only man behaves with such
gratuitous folly. It is the price he has to pay
for being intelligent, but not, as yet, quite
intelligent enough.

ALDOUS HUXLEY (1894–1963)
English novelist

❧ I must believe in the Apostolic Succession, there being no other way of accounting for the descent of the Bishop of Exeter from Judas Iscariot.

SYDNEY SMITH (1771–1845)
English clergyman and essayist

❧ Many people think they have religion when they are merely troubled with dyspepsia.

ROBERT GREEN INGERSOLL (1833–1899)

❧ Conscience is the inner voice which warns
us that somebody may be looking.

H. L. MENCKEN (1880–1956)

❧ Patience: a minor form of despair,
disguised as a virtue.

AMBROSE BIERCE (1842–1914)
American writer and journalist

❧ He preys on his knees on Sunday and on
everybody else for the rest of the week.

ANONYMOUS

❧ Passionate hatred can give meaning and purpose to an empty life.

ERIC HOFFER
English Labour politician

❧ What do you get if you cross a Jehovah's Witness with a biker?
   Some who knocks on your door and tells *you* to piss off.

ANONYMOUS

❧ The great thing about being Jewish is that you get more mileage out of your sins.

ANONYMOUS

❧ Catholics are so obsessed by sin, and so thrilled when they commit it, that one of the confessional boxes in St Peters is marked 'Eight Items or Less.'

ANONYMOUS

❧ I have nothing against the Jesuits but I wouldn't want my daughter to marry one.

PATRICK MURRAY

❧ An atheist is a man who has no invisible means of support.

JOHN BUCHAN (1875–1940)
Scottish writer and historian

∼ At a meeting of the Anglican synod called to discuss the proposition that the meek would inherit the earth, the meek decided they didn't want to.

ANONYMOUS

∼ Actually there were originally four wise men planning to attend the birth of Christ, but on the way to the manger, one of them said he knew a short-cut.

ANONYMOUS

❧ It is no accident that the symbol of a bishop is a crook and the sign of an archbishop is a double cross.

DOM GREGORY DIX
twentieth-century American theologian

❧ The people regarded as moral luminaries are those who forego ordinary pleasures themselves and find compensation in interfering with the pleasures of others.

BERTRAND RUSSELL (1873–1970)
British philosopher

❧ I don't think God comes well out of it.

VIRGINIA WOOLF (1882–1941)
English novelist, on The Book of Job

❧ I have no faith, very little hope, and as much charity as I can afford.

T. H. HUXLEY (1825–1895)
English biologist

❧ For two thousand years Christianity has been telling us: life is death, death is life; it is high time we consulted the dictionary.

EDMOND DE GOURMONT

❧ Organized Christianity has probably done more to retard the ideals that were its founder's than any other agency in the world.

RICHARD LE GALLIENNE (1866–1947)
English critic and contributor
to the Yellow Book

❧ The puritans hated bear-baiting, not because it gave pain to the bear but because it gave pleasure to the spectators.

THOMAS BABINGTON, LORD MACAULAY
(1800–1858)
English historian and poet

ॐ We must respect the other fellow's religion,
but only in the sense that we respect his
theory that his wife is beautiful and his
children smart.

H. L. MENCKEN (1880–1956)

ॐ God is the celebrity author of the world's
bestseller.
  We have made God into the biggest
celebrity of them all, to contain our own
emptiness.

DANIEL BOORSTIN (1914–)
author and historian

The toils of tourism

ଶ Frinton-on-Sea is so dull that it carries a
Government Health Warning. The town
caused hilarity by issuing a tourist brochure.

GEOFFREY ATKINSON
The I Hate Tourists Guide Book

ଶ EROS [*in Piccadilly Circus*] – the seedy
Greek God of Love surrounded by
prostitutes, drug addicts, drunks
and frightened Japanese tourists.

A LOCAL'S OBSERVATION

❧ Carnaby Street hasn't changed a bit. Still horrible. At obscene mark-ups it sells a fancy dress version of absurd sixties tat made in wretched Indonesian sweatshops.

❧ The motorway service station: sit up to your ankles in rubbish at a greasy table with a disc of emulsified offal, a stale bun, tea in polystyrene cup and a sachet of non-biodegradable milk – all for only ten pounds.

❧ At an unclean restaurant remember to say to the waiter: this table-cloth is filthy. Did you take it off your bed?

❧ Faced with slow service, try this engaging remark:

You British have never understood the meaning of work. That's why you lost an empire and became degenerate bum-bandits, isn't it?

Or

I'm sorry to see that all your waiters have died.

Or

Don't worry about me. Continental drift will soon carry me home.

❧ OXFORD STREET – a two-mile obstacle course of rude locals, hard-faced teenage pickpockets, privatised buses driven by psychopaths, and cheesy shops, many advertising 'Sales' with signs that have been in place since Roman times. Avoid at all costs.

❧ LONDON: *a Yuletide Salute*
Muggers grin as daylight fades,
Pukefalls line each filthy street,
Santa's coming down with AIDS –
Christmas here's a ****ing treat.

NICK AUSTIN (1944–)
English editor

∽ Things to say when asked 'Do you know the way to . . . ' by lost tourists:

'Yes I do. Thank you for asking.'

Or

'What? What? I can't understand your stupid accent. English is the language of God and Shakespeare. If you can't be arsed to speak properly, why should I bother?'

Or

'Sorry. I'm a stranger here myself . . . '

Or

[*Shouting*] 'I don't understand a word you're saying.'

Or

'Give us your travellers' cheques and piss off home, you Froggy/Kraut/Polak/Limey/ Wop/ Cloggy/Dago/Greaseball/Yank/Nip . . . '
[Depending on rough guess of nationality. No matter if you get it wrong – they are only tourists after all.]

Or

'Do you need to get there today?'

Or

'Of course you're starting at the wrong place . . . '

Or

'First left, second right, straight on for a mile,
    bear left at the sign of the Old Bollock Wort
    Pub, under the bridge, third left, and keep
    left for Christ's sake, through the market,
    hard right and you're there. Only a moron
    could miss it. Good bye.'

Curses for all
occasions

⚮ Woe to you that are mighty to drink wine,
and stout men at drunkenness.

ISAIAH 5:22

⚮ May thy emissions never exist.

EGYPTIAN CURSE
The Book of Ghastly Curses

⚮ May you have the runs on your
wedding night.

TRADITIONAL IRISH CURSE

⚮ If you die from fright, your soul will
be farting.

SERBIAN CURSE

      . . . for him may the thinkable become unthinkable, the easy difficult, practical aims unachievable, the productive unproductive, the cornfields barren, the fertile infertile, the sweet bitter, the fortunate unfortunate, the bright dark, the happy full of grief, and birthdays a matter of grief.

> ANCIENT CURSE AGAINST ROBBERS
> *inscribed on a tomb at Salamis, Cyprus*

       God send my enemies a celibate life.

> OVID (48 BC–AD 17)
> *Roman poet,* Amores

❧ For him that steals or borrows and returns
not this book, let it change into a serpent in
his hand and rend him. Let him be struck
with palsy and all his members blasted . . .
Let bookworms gnaw his entrails in the
token of the Worm that dieth not . . .

Written in a Bible,
Monastery of San Pedro, Barcelona

❧ May the sky over them be made of brass
and the earth underfoot of iron so that the
heavens will be unable to receive their souls
and earth unable to receive their bodies.

Excommunication text discovered
at the Abbey of Fécamp

✷ Let him be damned in his going out and
  coming in. The Lord strike him with
  madness and blindness. May the heavens
  empty upon him thunderbolts and the
  wrath of the Omnipotent burn itself unto
  him in the present and future world. May
  the Universe light against him and the
  earth open to swallow him up.

Wording of excommunication
from Pope Clement VI

✷ Hit your head on a corner of tofu and die!

JAPANESE CURSE

✷ The Pus of a poxy fox on your Whiskey.

IRISH CURSE

❧ May you wander forever in the company of
     crashing literary bores
  And be afflicted with the world's worst case
     of piles.

Priapea 41

❧ You scullion! Your rampallian! You
     fustilarian!
  I'll tickle your catastrophe!

WILLIAM SHAKESPEARE (1564–1616)
English dramatist, Henry IV Part 2

❧ May the Devil's dowser dip his twig in
  your buttermilk.

IRISH CURSE

␛ Die, may he: Tiger, catch him; Snake, bite him; Steep hill, fall down on him; River, flow over him; Wild boar, bite him.

RITUAL CURSE
from the Todas of India

␛ May the fleas of a thousand camels infest your armpits.

ARAB CURSE

␛ May beets grow in your navel so you piss borscht!

YIDDISH CURSE

 ❧ In church your grandsire cut his throat;
   To do the job too long he tarried:
   He should have had my hearty vote
   To cut his throat before he married.

JONATHAN SWIFT (1667–1745)
English satirist

 ❧ May your ears turn into arseholes and shit
   all over your shoulders.

AUSTRALIAN CURSE

 ❧ May you spend your days burning tarred
   rope in a bucket and squatting on it.

IRISH CURSE
describing treatment for piles

☍ May she marry a ghost, and bear him a kitten, and may the High King of Glory permit it to get the mange.

JAMES STEPHENS (1882–1950)
Irish poet

☍ No, I am not dead, and I would like to imprint proof of my unequivocal existence on your shoulders with a very vigorous stick. I would do so, in fact, did I not fear the plague miasma of your nephritic corpse.

MARQUIS DE SADE (1740–1814)
French writer, responding to an unflattering
premature obituary

❧ GR–r–r there go, my heart's abhorrence!
   Water your damned flower–pots, do!
If hate killed men, Brother Lawrence,
   God's blood, would not mine kill you!
What? Your myrtle-bush wants trimming?
   Oh, that rose has prior claims –
Needs its leaden vase filled brimming?
   Hell dry you up with its flames!

ROBERT BROWNING (1812–1889)
English poet, 'Soliloquy of the Spanish Cloister'

❧ May you be born in an important time.

CONFUCIUS (551–479 BC)
Chinese philosopher

☋ May you wander over the face of the earth
forever, never sleep twice in the same bed,
never drink water twice from the same
well, and never cross the same river
twice in a year.

GYPSY CURSE

☋ I shall consider you dead until the day
that prostitute's body which
resembles yours dies.

JEAN MOUNET–SULLY
nineteenth-century French actor, to
Sarah Bernhardt

Logorrhoea and buccal effusions

ꕥ There are few wild beasts more to be dreaded than a talking man having nothing to say.

JONATHAN SWIFT (1667–1745)
English writer

ꕥ She was a professional athlete – of the tongue.

ALDOUS HUXLEY (1894–1963)
English writer

ꕥ Your lips are like wet liver.

ꕥ Turn the ignition off, your mouth is still running

✌ I'll let you have the last word if you
  guarantee it will be your last.

✌ You've got a big hole in your head, now
  shut it.

✌ When you are at a loss for words, your
  loss is our gain.

✌ For pity's sake stop talking for a second so I
  can see what a compulsive Tourette's
  Syndrome lame-brain actually looks
  like in repose.

ও If you knew what you're talking about
you'd be dangerous.

ও You give away a lot of free advice, and only
charge what it's worth. You're a free thinker.
Your thoughts aren't worth anything.

ও He is the only person who enters the room
mouth first.

ও It's always difficult to follow an outstanding
speaker. Fortunately, I don't have that
problem tonight.

  ❧ If he ever had to eat his words, he'd put on fifteen pounds.

  ❧ I wish you were on TV – so I could turn you off.

  ❧ You should be wired for silence.

  ❧ In your case I see that the balance of power never moved northwards from your arse to your brain.

❧ You talk so much shit, you could plant a forest in it.

❧ English is your second language, isn't it? What a shame you don't have a first.

❧ Did you come up with that yourself, or do you owe all the credit to the many screaming voices in your head?

- If you ever waste my time again with another one of these sonnets to your stupidity, I will uppercut your jaw so hard that your head snaps backward and then snaps forward in perfect synchronicity for me to head butt you into a seven-year coma.

- If I want your stupid opinion, I'll beat it out of you.

- If I want any shit out of you I'll squeeze your head.

❧ You could just have easily have said
   that by burping.

❧ Shut up, before I slap you on the back of
   your head and send your brain rattling
   around like a pea in a whistle.

❧ Rearrange these two words into a well-
   known phrase: up shut.

❧ Take a deep breath and hold it until
   somewhere the end of *Tristan and Isolde*.

- If I want your opinion, I'd twist your ear and feed you a gumball, dimwit.

- Shut up, you hollerin' Redneck afflicted with Tourette's syndrome!

- Cackling like a hen that just jumped up on the dinner table doesn't help you gain respect around here.

- Take 55 milligrams of pure Diazepam and 120mg of Valium and sit in the corner and fondle yourself until the presence of a somewhat pacified braying jackass is requested.

❧ Climb back into your possum hole and don't pop your pointy-head up again; in case I decide Groundhog Day came early and wallop it with a baseball bat, you clodhopping yokel.

Pitfall personalities

❧ He would stab his best friend for the sake of writing an epigram on his tombstone.

OSCAR WILDE (1856–1900)
British dramatist and poet

❧ He is a fine friend. He stabs you in the front.

LEONARD LOUIS LEVINSON

❧ Bette Davis and I are good friends. There's nothing I wouldn't say to her face – both of them.

TALLULAH BANKHEAD (1903–1968)
American actress

❧ He was trying to save both his faces.

JOHN GUNTHER

❧ If I was two-faced, would I be wearing
this one?

ABRAHAM LINCOLN (1809–1865)
American president

❧ When he donates money to charity, he likes
to remain anonymous – so he doesn't sign
his name on the check.

ANONYMOUS

❧ She proceeds to dip her little fountain-pen filler into pots of oily venom and to squirt the mixture at all her friends.

HAROLD NICHOLSON (1886–1968)
British diplomat and writer

❧ A great many open minds should be closed for repairs.

TOLEDO BLADE NEWSPAPER

❧ He's the only man I ever knew who had rubber pockets so he could steal soup.

WILSON MIZNER

❧ He wears, almost everywhere, two faces;
   and you have scarce begun to admire
   the one, e'er you despise the other.

JOHN DRYDEN (1631–1700)
English poet, on William Shakespeare

❧ Has it ever occurred to you that there might
   be a difference between having an open
   mind and having holes in one's head?

RICHARD SCHULTZ

❧ What contemptible scoundrel stole the cork
from my lunch?

W. C. FIELDS (1880–1946)
American comic actor

❧ I drink too much. The last time I gave a
urine sample it had an olive in it.

RODNEY DANGERFIELD

❧ His mind is open like his front door, but
there's never anybody at home.

ANONYMOUS

ℝ She not only expects the worst, but makes
the worst of it when it happens.

MICHAEL ARLEN

ℝ I'm prepared to take advice on leisure
from Prince Philip. He's a world expert
on leisure. He's been practising for
most of his adult life.

NEIL KINNOCK
British politician, on the Duke of Edinburgh

ℝ There's a new theory about the origins of
the Grand Canyon. Apparently this
Scotsman dropped a shilling . . .

❧ Some people pay a compliment as if
   they expected a receipt.

KIN HUBBARD

❧ Drunkenness is his best virtue, for he will be
   swine drunk, and in his sleep he does little
   harm, save to his bedclothes about him.

WILLIAM SHAKESPEARE (1564–1616)
English dramatist, All's Well That Ends Well

❧ You've got more faces than an oven full of
   Gingerbread men.

⚞ He has more faces than a clock factory.

⚞ I am a drinker with writing problems.

BRENDAN BEHAN (1923–1964)
Irish writer

⚞ He's so mean he told his children that Santa
Clause got killed in a traffic accident so he
wouldn't have to buy them presents.

ANONYMOUS

Beastly bequests & execrable epitaphs

❧ If all else fails, immortality can always
   be assured by spectacular error.

JOHN KENNETH GALBRAITH (1908–)
Canadian economist

❧ I leave my right hand, to be cut off after
   my death, to my son Lord Audley; in
   hopes that such a sight may remind
   him of his duty to God, after having
   so long abandoned the duty he
   owed to a father who once
   affectionately loved him.

PHILIP THICKNESSE, 1793

❧ I give to Elizabeth Parker the sum of £50, whom, through my foolish fondness, I made my wife; and who in return has not spared, most unjustly, to accuse me of every crime regarding human nature, save highway-robbery.

CHARLES PARKER, 1785

❧ Friend, in your epitaph I'm grieved
So very much is said:
One-half will never be believed
The other never read.

ANONYMOUS

❧ Here lies Aretino, Tuscan poet
Who spoke evil of everyone but God,
Giving the excuse, 'I never knew him.'

ANONYMOUS

❧ A zealous locksmith died of late,
And did arrive at heaven's gate.
He stood without and would not knock,
Because he meant to pick the lock.

ANONYMOUS

❧ Here lies my wife: here let her lie!
Now she's at rest, and so am I.

JOHN DRYDEN (1631–1700)
English poet

⚞ Here lies our mutton-loving King
  Whose word no man relies on.
  Who never said a foolish thing,
  And never did a wise one.

JOHN, EARL OF ROCHESTER (1647–1680)
courtier and poet, on Charles II

CHARLES'S RESPONSE: True, for my words are
my own, but my deeds are my ministers'.

⚞ Under this stone, Reader, survey
  Dead Sir John Vanbrugh's house of clay.
  Lie heavy on him, Earth! for he
  Laid many heavy loads on thee!

DR ABEL EVANS

    I laid my wife
    Beneath this stone
    For her repose –
    And for my own.

ANONYMOUS, OTTAWA

Here lies the body of William Jay
Who died defending his right of way.
He was right, dead right, as he sped along
But he's just as dead as if he'd been

                 dead wrong.

ANONYMOUS

   ❧ Here lies a little ugly nauseous elf,
      Who judging only from its wretched self,
      Feebly attempted, petulant and vain,
      The 'Origin of Evil' to explain.

ANONYMOUS
on Soame Jenyns

   ❧ Sam Johnson: Reader, have a care,
      Tread lightly, lest you wake a sleeping bear;
      Religious, moral, generous and humane
      He was: but self-sufficient, proud and vain.
      Fond of, and overbearing in, dispute,
      A Christian and a scholar – but a brute.

SOAME JENYNS (1704–1787)
on Dr Samuel Johnson

❧ Bright ran thy line, O Galloway,
   Thro' many a far-fam'd sire;
   So ran the far-fam'd Roman way,
   So ended in a mire!

ROBERT BURNS (1759–1796)
Scottish poet, on Lord Galloway

❧ O reader behold the philosopher's grave!
   He was born quite a fool but he died quite a
      knave.

WILLIAM BLAKE (1757–1827)
English poet, artist and mystic, on
Sir Joshua Reynolds

❧ Died in Vermont the profane and
Impious Deist Gen. Ethan Allen . . .
And in Hell he lift up his eyes,
                                    being in Torments.

EZRA STILES (1727–1795)

❧   Posterity will ne'er survey
A nobler grave than this.
Here lie the bones of Castlereagh:
Stop, traveller and ——

GEORGE GORDON, LORD BYRON (1788–1824)
English poet

Here lies Fred,
Who was alive and is dead:
Had it been his father,
I had much rather;
Had it been his brother,
Still better than another;
Had it been his sister,
No one would have missed her;
Had it been the whole generation,
Still better for the nation:
But since 'tis only Fred,
Who was alive and is dead –
There's no more to be said.

ANONYMOUS
on Frederick, Prince of Wales (1707–1751)

❧ Here lies the father of taxation:
May Heaven, his faults forgiving,
Grant him repose; which he, while living,
Would never grant the nation.

R. A. DAVENPORT
on Jean Baptiste Colbert

❧ Here lies that peerless paper peer
     Lord Peter,
Who broke the laws of God and man
     and metre.

SIR WALTER SCOTT (1771–1832)
Scottish novelist and poet, on
Patrick Lord Robertson

       Hotton
       Rotten
       Forgotten

GEORGE AUGUSTUS HENRY SALA (1828–1895)
English novelist; epitaph for
John Camden Hotton

Under this stone does William Hazlitt lie
Thankless of all that God or man could give
He lived like one who never thought to die,
He died like one who dared not hope to live.

SAMUEL TAYLOR COLERIDGE (1772–1834)
English poet

    Here Lies
    Ezekial Aikle
    Aged 102
    The Good
    Die Young

ANONYMOUS

 Here richly, with ridiculous display,
  The Politician's corpse was laid away.
  While all of his acquaintance sneered
          and slanged,
  I wept: for I had longed to see him hanged.

HILAIRE BELLOC (1870–1953)
Anglo-French writer and poet

℞ Excuse my dust.

DOROTHY PARKER (1893–1967)
American writer – a proposed epitaph

℞ Poor G. K. C., his day is past –
Now God will know the truth at last.

E. V. LUCAS
proposed epitaph for G. K. Chesterton

℞ With death doomed to grapple
Beneath this cold slab, he
Who lied in the Chapel
Now lies in the Abbey.

GEORGE GORDON, LORD BYRON (1788–1824)
English poet, on William Pitt

❧ Lay aside, all yet dead
   For in the next bed
   Reposes the body of Cushing;
   He has crowded his way
   Through the world, as they say,
   And even though dead will keep pushing.

Epitaph proposed by Hanna F. Gould
on politician Caleb Cushing

❧ Here lies the mother of children seven
   Four on earth and three in heaven;
   The three in heaven preferring rather
   To die with mother than live with father.

ANONYMOUS

the bones of Robert Lowe:
ere he's gone to I don't know.
the realms of peace and love,
Farewell to happiness above.
If he's gone to a lower level,
I can't congratulate the Devil.

E. KNATCHBULL-HUGESSEN

❧ There lies beneath this mossy stone
A politician who
Touched a live issue without gloves,
And never did come to.

KEITH PRESTON

 ⅋ (*Wished at a Garden Party, June, 1.*
    I wish I loved the Human Race;
    I wish I loved its silly face;
    I wish I liked the way it walks;
    I wish I liked the way it talks;
    And when I'm introduced to one
    I wish I thought What Jolly Fun!

       PROFESSOR WALTER RALEIGH (1861–1922)
                 English scholar

 ⅋   Papa loved mamma
      Mamma loved men
      Mamma's in the graveyard
      Papa's in the pen

         CARL SANDBURG (1878–1967)
              American poet

ॐ Epitaph: An inscription on a tomb,
showing that virtues acquired by death
have a retroactive effect.

AMBROSE BIERCE (1842–1914)
American writer and journalist

ॐ Some men give blood to their country;
others their spleen.

FRANK GELETT BURGESS (1866–1951)
American writer and illustrator

ॐ The rarest quality in an epitaph is truth.

HENRY THOREAU (1817–1862)
American author and naturalist

❧ The good old horse and buggy days: then you lived until you died and not just until you were run over.

WILL ROGERS (1879–1935)
American actor and humorist

❧ Epitaph: a belated advertisement for a line of goods that has been permanently discontinued.

IRVIN COBB (1874–1944)
American journalist and writer

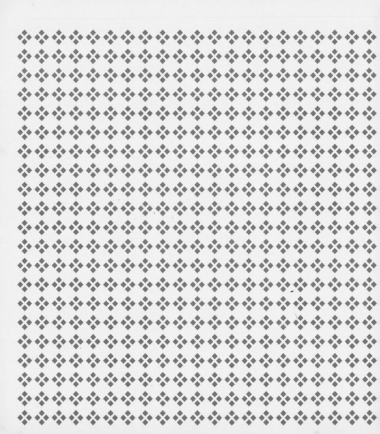